Men-at-Arms • 24

The Panzer Divisions

Martin Windrow • Illustrated by Richard Hook

Series editor Martin Windrow

First published in Great Britain in 1982 by
Osprey Publishing, Elms Court,
Chapel Way, Botley, Oxford OX2 9LP,
United Kingdom.
Email: info@ospreypublishing.com

Reprinted 1983, 1985 (twice), 1987, 1988, 1989, 1991,
1992, 1995, 1996 (three times), 1998, 1999, 2001, 2002, 2004 (twice)

CIP Data for this publication is available from the British Library

ISBN 0 85045 434 4

Series Editor: MARTIN WINDROW

Filmset in Great Britain
Printed in China through World Print Ltd.

FOR A CATALOGUE OF ALL BOOKS PUBLISHED BY
OSPREY MILITARY AND AVIATION PLEASE CONTACT:

The Marketing Manager, Osprey Direct UK,
PO Box 140, Wellingborough, Northants,
NN8 2FA, United Kingdom.
Email: info@ospreydirect.co.uk

The Marketing Manager, Osprey Direct USA,
c/o MBI Publishing, PO Box 1,
729 Prospect Avenue, Osceola, WI 54020, USA.
Email: info@ospreydirectusa.com

www.ospreypublishing.com

Introduction

I should at once confess that to call this book a 'revision' of the original title first published in 1973 is a fairly gross understatement. It is a different book entirely. In that first title I attempted to describe in at least brief detail not only the background to the formation of the German armoured units of the Second World War; not only to summarise their operations; not only to list the constituent units and main combat record of each division; but also to explain the uniforms of all the most important categories of troops which served within them. This was an act of madness, and my failure to achieve my aim was inevitable. This present title has a more modest goal.

The large number of general and specialist books published elsewhere in the past eight years on the history of the German armoured forces makes any attempt to cover the broader questions otiose. A selection of these titles, and several books explaining the general structure of German Army uniforms and insignia of the period, are listed in the bibliography, and readers are recommended to them without hesitation. I have avoided discussing or illustrating any uniforms not directly relevant to the officers and men of Army armoured units—tank, armoured car, assault artillery and self-propelled anti-tank regiments—and in all but three cases have limited my material to those uniforms and insignia actually worn in the combat zone. A more pedantically exact title for this book would be 'Uniforms of German Army Armoured Units 1935–45, with Notes on Divisional Assignment and Major Combat Deployments'; but there is a limit to the amount of headline type we can fit on the covers of this series, and I hope that readers will forgive me for taking the shifty way out and simply issuing it as 'The Panzer Divisions (Revised)'. The most obvious omission is any mention of the vital motorised and mechanised infantry component of the Panzer divisions—the Panzer-Grenadiers, without whom the tanks could not operate safely. To include them would involve a general survey of German infantry uniforms and equipment as a whole; once again, readers are directed to the bibliography and further reading list.

★ ★ ★

A Panzer company commander congratulates one of his NCOs on the award of the Iron Cross 2nd Class in Russia. The officer's rubber Wellingtons may not be particularly military-looking, but are highly practical winter wear.

'The office'—the cramped, crowded interior of a PzKpfw III tank, in which the crew fought, lived, ate, and slept. L to R: Looking left across gun breech at gunner's position; the same, with crew in place; driver's controls and vision block;

For the first three years of the war the German Army's armoured formations dominated the world's battlefields. During this period the shattering victories achieved by the Panzerwaffe paralysed enemies who were numerically stronger, and in some cases equipped with comparable or marginally superior tanks. The essence of this success lay in the characteristics and employment of the Panzer division, the creation of far-sighted leaders such as Guderian, Lutz and von Thoma.

The Allies were still hampered by an outmoded concept of armoured warfare, and by the inadequate equipment which had been produced to serve that concept. Broadly this may be described as the division of the function of the armour between the direct support of attacking infantry, which required heavy, slow tanks, and the rapid 'cavalry' evolutions which would turn flanks, scout ahead of the army, and exploit breakthroughs at speed, which required fast, light tanks. The war caught the Allies with inadequate numbers of obsolete tanks in both rôles; and from the first days the Panzerwaffe refused to play out the game foreseen by their bewildered enemies.

The Panzer division was a weapon of rapid attack. In classic form, once the lessons of Poland had been absorbed, it comprised a tank regiment; two regiments of infantry travelling in armoured personnel carriers and trucks; a reconnaissance battalion with armoured cars and half-tracks; an artillery regiment and an anti-tank battalion, at first equipped with towed guns but increasingly, as the war progressed, with a proportion of self-propelled guns on tracked chassis; and all necessary supporting services for rapid and independent advance. There was a generous allocation of radio equipment to allow commanders to co-ordinate the different arms in action; and close liaison with Luftwaffe ground-attack aircraft allowed them to call in air-strikes on pin-point targets, in place of the heavy artillery which the rapid advance of the Panzers had left behind. The tanks which formed the spearhead combined speed, armoured protection and gun-power to a degree far superior to the Allied designs, being all-purpose weapons generally capable of fighting targets of opportunity with high explosive, and other tanks with armour-piercing shot, with equal effectiveness. Unlike the Allies, the Germans set their tank soldiers apart from the start. They were specially selected; highly trained in more than one crew skill; and led by officers of audacious professional excellence. Their golden rules were, keep moving, and rely on what you have to hand. The formula was devastatingly effective.

The direct support firepower for the infantry attack—the guns which blew a path for the foot-soldier through the enemy blockhouses and

hull gunner/radio operator's position. Every cranny in a combat tank was crammed with equipment, spares, and ammunition, leaving little space for personal kit, much of which was stowed outside the vehicle.

machine gun positions—came from the separate Assault Artillery branch, equipped with tracked tank chassis mounting heavy guns in fixed armoured superstructures. As the tide of war turned against Germany these self-propelled guns were used more and more to reinforce the Panzers in the tank-vs-tank battle. Special self-propelled anti-tank guns—the Panzerjäger—were produced for this rôle. The assault guns and 'tank hunters' were allocated to the Panzer divisions in increasing numbers from 1942 onwards, but were more typically deployed in independent units under local control of Corps and Army commanders. The sweeping advances of 1940–42 became a memory, and the war turned into a grim defensive struggle for Germany; and with that change the 'SPs' came into their own even more markedly. Their large fixed superstructures could mount larger and longer-range guns than normally mounted in the complex revolving turret of a battle tank. In a defensive war of dug-in ambushers this lack of all-round traverse was no real handicap, and the longer reach of these weapons was a great advantage. Cheaper and easier to build than tanks, they had to a significant extent supplanted the Panzers—even in some nominally 'Panzer battalions'—by the end of the war.

Another type of unit deployed at Corps or Army level was the Heavy Tank Battalion, equipped with Tigers and King Tigers. These monsters, mounting the huge 88mm gun and so thickly armoured as to be invulnerable to Allied weapons under most conditions, were too slow and fuel-thirsty to be realistic weapons of fast, flexible attack. They were incorporated into some élite Panzer divisions such as the Army's 'Grossdeutschland', the Luftwaffe's 'Hermann Göring' and the three senior Waffen-SS tank divisions; but most were allocated to Corps units.

These are the units whose deployment and uniforms are touched upon in this book. For more detailed examination of their organisation and equipment, see the bibliography and further reading list.

The special quality of the German armoured units was evident not only during the early years of lightning victory. Right up to the end the Panzers remained a most potent weapon; even when outnumbered by tens to one, under skies ruled by swarming enemy aircraft, and fighting their last-ditch battles inside the shattered Reich, they were still capable of inflicting massively disproportionate losses on the advancing Shermans and T-34s. It is no accident that the image they create in the public consciousness, even 40 years later, is so powerful. A handful of types of military hardware or unit born of the Second World War have imprinted themselves on the memory of later generations so firmly that their names still conjure up a picture immediately understood and shared across the boundaries of time and nationality. Among them are 'Spitfire'; 'U-Boat'; 'Commando'; 'Stuka'; 'Flying Fortress'; 'Tiger tank'—and 'Panzer Division'.

The Divisions

The following note-form summaries show the bare bones of the history of the Panzerwaffe. Note that the English convention is used for dates, e.g. '1.12.43' = 1 December 1943, *not* 12 January 1943. Where a month and year are shown e.g. '1.44–', the meaning is 'from January 1944 onwards'. Only the most major actions are mentioned by name; the Panzer formations were almost continuously engaged when serving in Russia. In a few cases particularly well-known divisional commanders are shown. The heading 'MCUs' indicates major combat units of the division. Where the designations changed drastically—e.g. from Schützen-Regiment (Sch.Regt., 'Rifle Regt.') to Panzer-Grenadier-Regiment; or in cases where the division started its career with two tank regiments, later reduced; or where re-formation of a decimated division involved completely different units—the MCUs at more than one date are listed. Several divisions were formed from 'Light Divisions' (shown as e.g. '2.Lte.Div.') or from other existing combat formations, and these cases are indicated; where a division was raised from training and replacement pool in the normal way, or from reserve units, these are not specified.

1.Panzer-Division

Formed Weimar, 15.10.35, from parts 5.Kav.Div. Fought Poland, 9.39. With Pz.Gr.Kleist 5.40: Ardennes, Sedan. With Pz.Gr.Guderian 10.6.40–. With 4.Pz.Gr. on N. Russian front, 6.–10.40: Leningrad. To 3.Pz.Gr., central sector; Wiasma, Moscow. Fought around Rzhev, '42. Refitted France, 1.–6.43. In Greece, 7.–10.43. 11.–12.43, with 4.Pz.Arm.; fought W of Kiev. Defensive combat SW of Berdichev – 1.44. Counterattacked with 48.Pz.Kps. at Oleyyor on S flank of major Soviet breakthrough, 7.44. From Vistula front to Hungary, 10.44; defensive combat, counterattacks, Hungary/Austria, partic. at Dèbrecen, –4.45; surrendered to US forces E. Austria 5.45.
MCUs: 8.39: Pz.Regts.1, 2; Schützen Regt.1; Art.Regt.73; Aufkl.Abt.(mot)4; most div. units numbered 37. *10.40,* Pz.Regt.2 to 16.Pz.Div.; *11.40,* Sch.Regt.113 added. *'43:* Pz.Regt.1; Pz.Gren.Regts.1, 113; Pz.Aufkl.Abt.1; Art.Regt. 73.

2.Panzer-Division

Formed Wurzburg, 15.10.35. To Vienna, '38. Poland, 9.39; France, 5.–6.40. Polish occupation, 9.40–2.41. 4.–5.41, Balkans, Greece. Briefly SW France, then central sector Russia 9.41–: Moscow. Combat in Russia' 42–'43: Smolensk, Orel, Kiev, Dnieper. Refitted Amiens, France, after heavy losses, early '44. Heavy combat Normandy, 6.–8.44; nearly annihilated. Re-formed Wittlich, 9.44; led S element Ardennes offensive, 12.44. Defensive combat Rhine front, early '45; surrendered Plauen, 5.45.
MCUs: '39: Pz.Regts.3, 4; Sch.Regt.2; Art. Regt.74; most div. units numbered 38. *9.40,* Pz.Regt.4 to 13.Pz.Div. *'43:* Pz.Regt.3; Pz.Gren. Regts.2, 304; Pz.Aufkl.Abt.2; Art.Regt.74.

3.Panzer-Division

Formed Wünsdorf, Berlin, 15.10.35. Poland, 9.39; France, 5.–6.40. Several MCUs to 5.Lte.Div., Germany, 1.41; units from several divs. added. 6.41–2.42, Russia, with 2.Pz.Gr., Arm.Gp.Centre. 2.–3.42, to S sector; advanced Caucasus summer '42; heavy losses Mozdok, 11.–12.42. Heavy combat Kharkov, summer '43; Dnieper Bend, 9.43–1.44. Defensive combat Ukraine, Poland, '44. To Hungary 1.45; retreated Austria 4.45; surrendered to US forces at Steyr, 5.45.
MCUs: '39: Pz.Regts.5, 6; Sch.Regt.3; Art. Regt.75; Aufkl.Abt.(mot)3; most div. units numbered 39. *'43:* Pz.Regt.6; Pz.Gren.Regts.3, 394; Pz.Aufkl.Abt.3; Art.Regt.75. (COs incl. Gen.Lt. Model, 11.40–10.41; Gen.Maj. Bayerlein, 10.43–1.44.)

4.Panzer-Division

Formed Würzburg, 10.11.38. Fought Poland, 9.39; France, 5.–6.40. Russian front, Arm.Gp. Centre, 6.41–. Caucasus, '42; N element Kursk offensive, 7.43; defensive combat Gomel, 8.–9.43, and on central front winter '43–'44. To Latvia

summer '44; Kurland 1.45; W. Prussia, surrendered to Soviets 4.45.
MCUs: 8.39: Pz.Regts.35, 36; Sch.Regt.12; Art.Regt.103; Aufkl.Abt.(mot)7; most div. units numbered 79. *10.–11.39,* Pz.Regt.36 to 14.Pz. Div.; Sch.Regt.33 added. *'43:* Pz.Regt.35; Pz. Gren.Regts.12, 33; Pz.Aufkl.Abt.4; Art.Regt. 103; Pz.Jäg.Abt.49.

5.Panzer-Division

Formed Oppeln, 24.11.38. Fought Poland, 9.39; prominent in France, 5.–6.40. Invaded Yugoslavia, Greece, 4.41. Heavy combat central sector Russia, 6.41–. Demjansk, early '43; heavy losses Kursk, 7.43; Dnieper, '44. To Latvia, 7.44; Kurland, 8.–10.44; E.Prussia, 11.44. Hela Peninsula, 3.45; surrendered to Soviets 4.45.
MCUs: '38: Pz.Regts.15, 31; Sch.Regts.13, 14; Aufkl.Abt.(mot)8; Art.Regt.116; Pz.Abw.Abt. 53; variously numbered div.units. *9.40:* Pz.Regt. 15 to 11.Pz.Div. *'43:* Pz.Regt.31; Pz.Gren.Regts. 13, 14; Pz.Aufkl.Abt.5; Art.Regt.116.

6.Panzer-Division

Formed Wuppertal, 18.10.39, from 1.Lte.Div. which fought in Poland, 9.39. Fought in West, 5.–6.40. With 4.Pz.Gr. on N sector of Russian front, 6.41: Leningrad. To 3.Pz.Gr., central sector, 10.41, where nearly wiped out winter '41–'42. Survivors to France, 5.42; to S sector Russian front, 12.42; attempted to relieve Stalingrad. Combat around Kharkov, early '43; Belgorod, S element of Kursk attacks, 7.43. Defensive combat winter '43; heavy losses 3.44; refitted, fought on central sector throughout Soviet summer offensive. To Hungary, 12.44; defence of Budapest; retreated Austria 3.45, combat around Vienna. Surrendered to Soviets at Brno, 5.45.
MCUs: '39: Pz.Regt.11, Pz.Abt.65; Sch.Regt.4; Pz.Abw.Abt.41; Art.Regt.76; most div. units numbered 57. *'42:* Pz.Regt.11; Pz.Gren.Regts.4, 114; Pz.Aufkl.Abt.6; Pz.Abw.Abt.41; Art.Regt. 76.

7.Panzer-Division

Formed Gera, 18.10.39, from 2.Lte.Div. which fought in Poland, 9.39. Distinguished in West, 5.–6.40. Heavily engaged 7.41–5.42, central sector Russian front with 3.Pz.Gr.; refitted France; occupation Vichy sector, 11.42. To S sector Russian front, winter '42–'43; combat Kharkov,

Autumn 1940: company briefing for crews of Pz-Regt.11, 6.Pz-Div.—identifiable by the cupola of a Czech-built PzKpfw 35(t) tank in background, as this was the only unit which operated these vehicles. The officer is probably either Hptm. Erich Löwe or Oblt.Erich Bethke, both of whom received the Knight's Cross on 4 September 1940. (Imperial War Museum)

spring '43. Combat Belgorod, S element Kursk offensive, 7.43; with 4.Pz.Arm. at Kharkov, summer '43; Kiev, Zhitomir; heavy losses 11.43. Retreated N.Ukraine, 3.44; defensive combat during Soviet summer offensive. To Baltic, 8.44, with 3.Pz.Arm. Lithuania, Kurland, Memel, late '44. Heavy combat W of Vistula 1.45; withdrew into Prussia; surrendered to British, Schwerin, 5.45.
MCUs: 4.40: Pz.Regt.25, Pz.Abt.66; Sch.Regts. 6, 7; Pz.Jäg.Abt.42; Art.Regt.78; most div. units numbered 58. *'43:* Pz.Regt.25; Pz.Gren.Regts.6, 7; Pz.Aufkl.Abt.7; Pz.Jäg.Abt.42; Art.Regt.78. (COs incl. Gen.Maj.Rommel, 2.40–2.41; Gen. Maj.Hasso Frhr.von Manteuffel, 8.43–1.44.)

8.Panzer-Division

Formed Cottbus, 16.10.39, from 3.Lte.Div. which fought in Poland, 9.39. Fought 5.–6.40 in France; occupation of Yugoslavia, 4.41, but no combat. With 4.Pz.Gr. on N.Russian front, 7.41; Leningrad. 3.–11.42 in action Cholm; 12.42–2.43, Smolensk. 4.–8.43 heavily engaged Orel, incl. N element Kursk offensive; heavy losses in withdrawal W of Kiev. 10.43. With 4.Pz.Arm. on S sector, 1.–9.44: Zhitomir, Tarnopol, Brody, Lemberg. 9.44, to Carpathians; defence Budapest, 12.44 Defensive fighting in Moravia, 2.–3.45; surrendered to Soviets, Brno, 5.45.

The high tide of victory: a PzKpfw IV Ausf.F tank of 11.Pz-Div.—the 'Ghost Division'—supports divisional infantry during the advance into south Russia in summer 1941.

MCUs: 4.40: Pz.Regt.10, Pz.Abt.67; Sch.Regt.8; Pz.Jäg.Abt.43; Art.Regt.80; most div. units numbered 59. *'43:* Pz.Regt.10; Pz.Gren.Regts.8, 28; Pz.Aufkl.Abt.8; Pz.Jäg.Abt.43; Art.Regt.80.

9.Panzer-Division

Formed 3.1.40, from 4.Lte.Div. which fought in Poland, 9.39. Fought Netherlands, France, 5.–6.40; Antwerp, Brussels, Arras, Dunkirk, Amiens, Lyons. With 12.Arm., Balkans, spring '41. To S sector Russian front, 7.41; to central sector, 10.41, and throughout '42. Took part N element Kursk fighting, 7.43; defensive fighting, Dnieper Bend, autumn '43, on S sector of front. Heavy losses winter '43–'44; to France 3.44, brought to strength with 155.Pz.Res.Bde. To invasion front, 8.44: Falaise. Withdrew to Aachen area, 9.44. With 5.Pz.Arm. in Ardennes, 12.44; in Eifel area with 15.Arm., 2.–3.45. Trapped in Ruhr Pocket; surrendered to US forces, 5.45.

MCUs: '40: Pz.Regt.33; Sch.Regts.10, 11; Aufkl. Abt.9; Pz.Jäg.Abt.50; Art.Regt.102; some div. units numbered 60. *'43:* Pz.Regt.33 'Prinz Eugen'; Pz.Gren.Regts.10, 11; Pz.Aufkl.Abt.9; Pz.Jäg. Abt.50; Art.Regt.102.

10.Panzer-Division

Formed Prague from 4.39 onwards. Part fought Poland, 9.39, as 'Pz.Verband Ostpreussen'. Div. fought in France, 5.–6.40. On central sector Russian front 6.41–4.42: Gzhatsk, Vyazma. 5.42 to France for refitting; took part operations against Allied landing Dieppe, 8.42; occupation Vichy sector 11.42; to Tunisia, 12.42, where annihilated, 5.43.

MCUs: 4.40: Pz.Regts.7, 8; Sch.Regts.69, 86; Art.Regt.90; most div. units numbered 90. *'43:* Pz.Regt.7; Pz.Gren.Regts.69, 86; Pz.Aufkl.Abt. 10; Art.Regt.90.

11.Panzer-Division

Formed 1.8.40, mainly from 11.Sch.Bde. which had fought in France. 4.41, invaded Balkans, captured Belgrade. 6.–7.41, to S sector Russian front; fought in central sector 10.41–6.42, returned to S front. Engaged at Orel, Belgorod, 7.43; heavy fighting Krivoi Rog, autumn '43. Heavy losses, Korsun Pocket, 1.–2.44. Remnant to S.France for refit, 6.44, incorporating 273.Res. Pz.Div. 8.–9.44, defensive combat in face Allied landings S.France, withdrawal to Alsace: Belfort

Gap. To Saar area. Combat in Ardennes, 12.44; with 7.Arm., Trier, 1.45. 3.45, combat at Remagen; surrendered to US forces, Bavaria, 5.45.
MCUs: Pz.Regt.15; Pz.Gren.Regts.110, 111; Pz.Aufkl.Abt.11; Art.Regt.119; most div. units numbered 61.

12.Panzer-Division
Formed Stettin, 5.10.40, from 2.Inf.Div.(mot). To central sector Russian front, 7.41: Minsk, Smolensk. 9.41 to N sector; heavy losses before Leningrad, winter '41. Withdrawn to Estonia for refit, 1.42; returned to Leningrad, continuous operations –11.42, when to Roslavl area of central front. 3.–8.43 in action Orel, Bryansk, Gomel; defensive combat on middle Dnieper in autumn. 2.44, to Leningrad, and subsequent withdrawal from siege lines. 8.44–, heavy fighting in Kurland; surrendered to Soviets 4.45.
MCUs: Pz.Regt.29; Pz.Gren.Regts.5, 25; Pz. Aufkl.Abt.12; Art.Regt.2; most div. units numbered 2.

13.Panzer-Division
Formed Vienna area, 11.10.40, from 13.Inf.Div. (mot); to Rumania as training formation. 6.41, took part in Russian invasion, S sector: capture of Kiev. Drove to Caucasus, summer '42; heavy fighting Terek, Taganrog. Winter '42–'43, engaged in Kuban. Withdrew spring '43 to Taman Peninsula, crossed to Crimea 7.43. Heavily engaged Krivoi Rog, 10.43–1.44. Spring–summer '44, withdrew across N.Ukraine, Rumania, to Carpathians; to Germany for refit, 9.44. To Hungary, 10.44; defended Budapest with 6.Arm., 11.–12.44; encircled; wiped out, 1.45. Re-formed at once as Pz.Div.'Feldherrnhalle 2', q.v.
MCUs: Pz.Regt.4; Pz.Gren.Regts.66, 93; Pz. Aufkl.Abt.13; Art.Regt.13; most div. units numbered 13.

14.Panzer-Division
Formed 15.8.40 from 4.Inf.Div. Engaged in Yugoslavia, 4.41. After refit, to S sector Russian front; continuously engaged 7.41–12.42. Encircled at Stalingrad, wiped out 1.43. Re-formed Brittany, 4.43–. Returned S sector Russian front 10.43; heavily engaged in Dnieper Bend, 12.43. Combat around Kirovograd, Kishinevo, Jassi areas, 1.–6.44. Refitted in Ukraine, 7.44; to Kurland, 8.44. Defensive fighting Libau area, 10.44–4.45, when surrendered to Soviets.
MCUs: Pz.Regt.36; Pz.Gren.Regts.103, 108; Pz.Aufkl.Abt.14; Art.Reg.4; most div. units numbered 4.

15.Panzer-Division
Formed 1.11.40 from 33.Inf.Div.; shipped to Libya as part of original Deutsches Afrika Korps, 2.41. As one of Rommel's two Panzer divisions, continuously engaged against British and Commonwealth forces throughout 1941–42, the survivors of El Alamein retreating to Tunisia in winter '42–'43. Virtually destroyed 4.–5.43, and surrendered with other Axis forces in Tunisia 12.5.43. Re-formed in Sicily, 7.43, originally as 'Div.Sizilien', later as 15.Pz.Gren.Div.
MCUs: Pz.Regt.8; Pz.Gren.Regt.115; Art.Regt. 33; most div.units numbered 33.

16.Panzer-Division
Formed 1.11.40 from 16.Inf.Div.; to Rumania as training formation, 12.40. Continuously engaged S sector Russian front 6.41–12.42: Lvov, Pervomaisk, Zaporozhe, Taganrog, Artemorsk, and finally Stalingrad, where div. encircled and wiped out 1.43. Re-formed, France, 3.43; to N.Italy, 6.43; fought Allied landings, Salerno, Naples, 9.–10.43. To central Russian front, 12.43. Heavy losses in '44 counterattack W of Kiev; withdrew to Vistula, Baranov area. After refitting in Poland, 10.44, defensive fighting, Baranov, Lauban, 3.–4.45. Surrendered at Brno, 4.45, part to US, part to Soviets.
MCUs: Pz.Regt.2; Pz.Gren.Regts.64, 79; Art. Regt.16; most div. units numbered 16.

17.Panzer-Division
Formed 1.11.40 from 27.Inf.Div.; continuously engaged on central Russian front 6.41–11.42. Took part, with 4.Pz.Arm., in attempt relieve Stalingrad. Summer–autumn '43, heavy fighting on Donets, in Dnieper Bend, in aftermath of German defeat at Kursk. Fought in all major actions during retreat N.Ukraine, 3.–8.44: Proskurov, Chortkov, Stanislav, to Chelm, Poland. 9.–12.44, operations Opatov, Chmielnik, Kielce. 1.45, remnants in defensive fighting around Soviet bridgehead, Baranov. 2.–3.45, withdrew W of Görlitz; overrun by Soviets, 4.45.
MCUs: Pz.Regt.39; Pz.Gren.Regts.40, 63; Pz.

Crews of either 15. or 21.Pz-Div. relax beside their PzKpfw III tanks in North Africa, 1941. The sun helmet was unpopular, as it was impossible to wear it inside the tank, and had to be slung outside the turret and retrieved when climbing out—a tiresome procedure.

Aufkl.Abt.17; Art.Regt.27; most div. units numbered 27. (COs incl. Gen.Lt. von Arnim, 10.40 and 9.–11.41; Gen.Maj.Ritter von Thoma, 7.–9.41; Gen.Maj.Frhr.von Senger u.Etterlin, 10.42–6.43.)

18.Panzer-Division

Formed 26.10.40, Chemnitz, from parts 4. & 14. Inf.Div.; continuously engaged, central Russian front, 6.41–6.42. Returned central sector after period in S; operations in Bryansk, Orel area, 9.43. Heavy fighting W of Kiev, 10.43, during German counteroffensive; div. inactivated after heavy losses, 20.10.43, withdrawn Orsha. Reorganised, Lithuania, as 18.Artillerie-Division.
MCUs: Pz.Abt.18; Pz.Gren.Regts.52, 101; Pz. Aufkl.Abt.18; Art.Regt.18; most div. units numbered 18.

19.Panzer-Division

Formed 1.11.40, mainly from 19.Inf.Div.; continuous operations on central Russian front 6.41–12.42; then to S sector. Heavy losses in Belgorod attack on S axis of Kursk offensive, 7.43. Defensive fighting, 9.43–6.44, during withdrawal N.Ukraine to Warsaw area: Kiev, Zhitomir, Shepetovka, Proskurov, Stanislav. Refitted, Holland, 6.–7.44. Defensive fighting, Poland, 8.–12.44. Fought around Baranov bridgehead, 1.–2.45, then Breslau, Silezice, with 1.Pz.Arm. To Bohemia, where surrendered 5.45.
MCUs: Pz.Regt.27; Pz.Gren.Regts.73, 74; Pz. Aufkl.Abt.19; Art.Regt.19; most div. units numbered 19.

20.Panzer-Division

Formed Erfurt, 15.10.40, from part 19.Inf.Div. Central Russian front, 6.41, advanced to Moscow area. Remained in central sector until 7.43, when attacked at Orel, N element of Kursk offensive. Withdrew Gomel, Orsha, Vitebsk, 10.–12.43. Defensive fighting Polotsk, Vitebsk, Bobruisk areas, 1.–4.44. To S sector, operations Cholm area, 5.44; heavy losses during Soviet summer offensive; to Rumania for refitting, 8.44. To E. Prussia, 10.44; to Hungary, 12.44. Defensive

fighting during retreat Breslau, Schweidnitz, Neisse, Görlitz; overrun by Soviets 5.45.
MCUs: Pz.Regt.21; Pz.Gren.Regts.59, 112; Pz. Aufkl.Abt.20; Pz.Art.Regt.92; most div. units numbered 92. (COs incl. Gen.Maj. Ritter von Thoma, 10.41–6.42; Gen.Maj. von Oppeln-Bronikowski, 11.44–5.45.)

21.Panzer-Division
Formed 1.8.41, in the field, from elements 5.Lte.Div. plus Pz.Regt.5 and other elements 3.Pz.Div. Since 2.41, operations N.Africa with DAK; all major campaigns in desert against British Commonwealth forces, '41–'42. Heavy losses Alam Halfa and El Alamein, 7. and 10.42. Provided rearguard for Axis retreat to Tripoli and Tunisia. Virtually annihilated, Tunis, 5.43, and surrendered. Re-formed, Normandy, 7.43; occupation duties, France, –6.44, when heavily engaged against Allied invasion and subsequent German withdrawal across France. Fighting retreat, Saar and N.Alsace; refitted, Germany; to Russian front, 2.45. Defended Lauban, Görlitz, Cottbus areas; overrun by Soviets, 4.45.
MCUs: '42: Pz.Regt.5; Pz.Gren.Regts.47, 104; Pz.Art.Regt.155; Pz.Aufkl.Abt.580; most div. units numbered 200. *'44:* Pz.Regt.22; Pz.Gren. Regts.125, 192; Pz.Aufkl.Abt.21; Pz.Art.Regt. 155.

22.Panzer-Division
Formed France, 25.9.41, and to central Russian front, 2.42. Heavily engaged Crimea, Kerch Peninsula, spring '42. Further heavy combat on Donets, Don, at Rostov, summer–autumn '42. Attempted to seal off Russian breakthrough at Kalach N of Stalingrad, 11.42: encircled and virtually wiped out. Survivors, notably Pz.Gren. Regt.129, withdrew to Starobelsk, Chistyakovo, 1.–3.43. Remnant redesignated 'KampfGr.Brugsthaler', 3.43; absorbed by 23.Pz.Div., 4.43.
MCUs: Pz.Regt.204; Pz.Gren.Regts.129, 140; Pz.Aufkl.Abt.140; Pz.Art.Regt.140; div. units numbered 140.

23.Panzer-Division
Formed Paris area, 9.41–3.42. To S sector Russian front, 4.42; heavily engaged in defeat Soviet attack Kharkov, 5.42. Drove into Caucasus, reached Terek river; 12.42, moved N to Stalingrad area, took part relief attempt with 4.Pz.Arm. To Bolshaya, Rostov, Stalino; defended in this area –7.43. Heavy defensive fighting 7.–12.43: Dnieper Bend, Kharkov, Krivoi Rog, Kremenchug, Kirovograd. Cited for defence Krivoi Rog area, 1.–3.44; Jassi, 4.–8.44. Refitted, and defensive operations, Poland, summer '44. To Hungary, 10.44; combat around Dèbrecen. Fighting retreat Hungary, Slovenia, to Graz area, Austria, 11.44–4.45; overrun by Soviets 5.45.
MCUs: Pz.Regt.23; Pz.Gren.Regts.126, 128; Pz.Aufkl.Abt.23; Pz.Art.Regt.128; most div. units numbered 128.

24.Panzer-Division
Formed 28.11.41 at Stablack, E.Prussia, from veteran 1.Kav.Div.; trained France, 4.–6.42; to S sector Russian front, where engaged 7.42–1.43, when encircled and wiped out at Stalingrad. Remnants to France, where div. re-formed 4.43. To Italy, 8.43, occupation duty. To S sector Russian front, 10.43; defensive fighting Nikopol, Krivoi Rog, Krasnograd; heavy losses. Continued heavy fighting, withdrawal Krivoi Rog, Jassi, 2.–4.44. Defensive fighting Jassi area during Soviet offensive S.Poland, 4.–8.44. To Hungary, 10.44; Slovakia, 12.44–1.45. Withdrew to E. Prussia, defensive fighting 2.–4.45. Withdrew into Schleswig–Holstein and surrendered to British, 5.45.
MCUs: Pz.Regt.24; Pz.Gren.Regts.21, 26; Pz. Aufkl.Abt.24; Pz.Art.Regt.89; most div. units numbered 40.

25.Panzer-Division
Formed Eberswalde, 25.2.42, then to Norway where incorporated troops from occupation force. To Denmark briefly, 8.43, then to France. 10.43 to S sector Russian front, W of Kiev. Defensive fighting, heavy losses, 12.43–4.44: Berdichev, Proskurov, Chortkov, Stanislav. 5.44, to Denmark for refitting. 9.44, to Pultusk, Poland; defensive combat Radom, Guben, Müncheberg, 10.44–2.45. Withdrew into Germany, overrun by Soviets 5.45.
MCUs: Pz.Regt.9; Pz.Gren.Regts.146, 147; Pz. Aufkl.Abt.87; Pz.Art.Regt.91; most div. units numbered 87.

26.Panzer-Division
Formed Mons, Belgium, 14.9.42, from 23.Inf.

Excellent study of an NCO (left) and officer of the Pz-Regt. 'Grossdeutschland'—the right sleeve cuff title is just visible. The NCO has the earlier uniform features—pink collar piping and pink soutache on the Feldmütze; the Leutnant—whose age and decorations clearly indicate a commissioned NCO with long service—wears the unpiped collar seen from 1943 onwards. Note silver officer's piping on his Feldmütze. (ECPA)

Div.; to Amiens area, 10.42. To Italy, 7.43; fought Salerno, Cassino areas. 1.–5.44, fought Anzio, Nettuno area. 6.–12.44, defensive fighting Orsogna, Frosinone, Rimini, Ravenna, Bologna. Imola area, 3.–4.45; surrendered 5.45.
MCUs: Pz.Regt.26; Pz.Gren.Regts.9, 67; Pz. Aufkl.Abt.26; Pz.Art.Regt.93; most div. units numbered 93.

27.Panzer-Division

Formed 1.10.42, Voronezh sector of S sector Russian front, from elements of 22.Pz.Div.; fought around Voronezh, Voroshilovgrad until disbanded 15.2.43, its units being absorbed by 7. and 24.Pz.Divs.
MCUs: Pz.Abt.127; Pz.Gren.Regt.140; Pz.Art. Regt.127; div. units numbered 127.

116.Panzer-Division

Formed France, 28.3.44 from 116.Pz.Gren.Div.; engaged throughout Normandy campaign and withdrawal through France. Refitted in defensive positions Aachen/Eifel area, 9.–11.44. With 5.Pz. Arm. in S element Ardennes offensive; heavy losses. To Kleve on Rhine, 1.45; surrendered to US forces in Ruhr, 4.45.
MCUs: Pz.Regt.16; Pz.Gren.Regts.60, 156; Pz. Aufkl.Abt.116; Pz.Art.Regt.146; Pz.Jäg.Abt.226; variously numbered div. units.

(130.) Panzer-Lehr-Division

Formed Potsdam, Bergen, from 11.43 from Panzer demonstration units of various armoured warfare schools. Brief transfers to France, Hungary, 2.–4.44; near Paris at D-Day, with very large establishment of AFVs (190 tanks, 40 StuG, 612 half-tracks) and unusually expert personnel. Very heavy combat Normandy, 6.–8.44: Caen, St.Lô. Reduced to 50 AFVs by withdrawal of 8.44; to Saar, then Paderborn; refitted. Fought Ardennes, 12.44; surrendered to US forces in Ruhr, 4.45.
MCUs: Pz.L.Regt.130; Pz.Gren.L.Regts.901, 902; Pz.Aufkl.L.Abt.130; Pz.Art.L.Regt.130; most div. units numbered 130. (COs incl. Gen.Lt. Fritz Bayerlein, Gen.Maj.Graf Strachwitz.)

Panzer-Division 'Grossdeutschland'

The history of this premier German Army armoured formation is covered in Vanguard 2, *Panzer-Division 'Grossdeutschland'*, by Bruce Quarrie, published by Osprey in 1977. For space reasons this complex story will not be summarised here, beyond noting that this very strong formation, steadily increased in establishment from a motorised infantry regiment to a Panzer-Korps, fought with distinction in France, 1940; the Balkans and Greece, 1941; on the Russian front, including the battles of Kharkov and Kursk, 1943; the Dnieper Bend; Kurland, 1944; and the final battles in E.Prussia, 1945. Its MCUs in 1944 included a Pz.Regt. of three bns. (III Btl. with Tiger tanks), two strong mechanised/motorised inf. regiments, a StuG-Bde., and strong supporting units, all un-numbered but bearing the honour title 'GD'. In the last part of the war certain other élite units were brought to battlefield status and designated as part of the 'Grossdeutschland Verbände', entitled to that formation's cuff title. These were:

Führer-Begleit-Division

Motorised infantry bodyguard unit from Hitler's HQ; raised to bde. strength '44, and heavily engaged in Ardennes, 12.44. Nominally upgraded to div. status 1.45; heavy defensive combat on Oder front; decimated near Spremberg, 4.45. Its MCUs incl. Pz.Regt., Pz.Gren.Regt., and Art.Abt., all with honour title.

Führer-Grenadier-Division
Raised after the Bomb Plot of 7.44, this bde. was based at Cottbus, near the Rastenburg HQ. Its MCUs incl. Pz.Gren.Regt., Fusilier Btl. and Pz.Abt. with honour title 'F-G-B'. Heavily engaged defensive combat E.Prussia 10.–12.44; then to West, Ardennes offensive. 2.45, nominally raised to div. status, with Pz.Regt., StuG.Bde., Pz.Gren.Bde.; to Stargard area, heavy fighting. 3.45, Stettin; later at Kustrin bridgehead. 4.45 to Vienna; surrendered to US forces but handed over to Soviets.

Panzer-Division 'Kurmark'
Formed Cottbus, 22.1.45, from remnants 'Kampf Gr. Langkeit'; CO was Oberst Langkeit, formerly of Pz.Regt.'GD', and new unit awarded 'GD' cuff title. Consisting of Pz.Regt., Pz.Gren. Regt., Pz.Art.Regt. and Pz.Aufkl.Regt. with div. units and services, all identified by honour title 'Kurmark', it was sent to Oder front 2.45. Heavy defensive fighting 2.–4.45. In Müncheberg area late 4.45; broke through encirclement at Halbe, crossed Elbe; survivors surrendered to US forces, 5.5.45.

Several other armoured formations existed 'on paper' at the end of the war, identified by honour titles such as 'Clausewitz', 'Holstein', 'Müncheberg', 'Schlesien', 'Jüterbog', etc. The only ones thought to have seen combat are:

Panzer-Division 'Feldherrnhalle 2'
Understrength formation formed 1.45 from remnants 13.Pz.Div. and 60.Pz.Gren.Div. 'Feldherrnhalle', both nearly wiped out at Budapest. Defensive fighting on retreat from Hungary to Austria, where it surrendered. CO in final months' fighting was Oberst Dr.Franz Bäke—see Plate Hl.

232.Panzer-Division ('Tatra')
Training unit redesignated as Pz.Div. 21.2.45; destroyed at Raab bridgehead, 3.45.

Schwere-Panzer-Abteilungen:
The following partial notes show general deployment of Tiger tank battalions:
sPz–Abt.501 Part to Tunisia, 11.42. In action Tebourba, 12.42; Hamra, 19.1.43; Faid/Kasserine area, 14.2.43. Heavy losses Hunt's Gap, 27.2.43. In action Maknassy, Medjerda Valley, 3.–4.43; surrendered 12.5.43. Re-formed: to Russia 12.43; in action Vitebsk area early '44. Refitted with King Tigers 7.44; continuous action Poland 8.–12.44: Radom, Sandomierz, Kielce. Became 24.Pz.Kps. unit 'Korps-Tiger-Abt.424', 12.44; destroyed 1.45.
sPz–Abt.502 To Leningrad front 8.42 (part); in action this sector –'44. Withdrew into Kurland: in action Riga, Memel, Königsburg, winter '44–'45. Surrendered E.Prussia 9.5.45; total confirmed kills for war incl. more than 2,000 Soviet tanks.
sPz–Abt.503 Held open Rostov gap for retreat Caucasus forces, winter '42–'43. On S axis Kursk offensive, 7.43. Fighting withdrawal over Dnieper, winter '43. To 'Pz.Regt.Bäke', 1.–3.44 (see under Plate H1). Refitted with King Tigers, France; into action against British E of Caen, 7.44. Inflicted heavy losses British attack Bourgeubus Ridge, but heavy casualties from air attack, 18.7.44. Heavy losses at Amiens. Refitted 9.44; to Hungary 10.44; defensive combat –5.45.
sPz–Abt.504 Part to Tunisia, 3.43. In action Maknassy, Medjerda, 3.–5.43; surrendered 5.43. Remainder in action Sicily; crossed to Italy. Abt. re-formed Holland, to Italy 6.44. Successful combat Parolla; in autumn/winter to Gothic Line, Rimini area; fought British until surrender 3.5.45.
sPz–Abt.505 On N axis Kursk attacks, 7.43; remained with Army Gp. Centre until collapse of summer '44; refitted with King Tigers; defensive fighting E.Prussia –5.45.
sPz–Abt.506 Fought with Army Gp.Centre 9.43–; Lemberg, Tarnopol. To West for refit, 8.44. In action Arnhem, Nijmegen, 9.44; Aachen, 11.44; Ardennes offensive, 12.44. Captured in Ruhr, 4.45.
sPz–Abt.507 With Army Gp.Centre, 3.44–; in action Tarnopol area. To N sector Russian front, 11.44, where in action until destroyed 4.45.
sPz–Abt.508 Formed 8.43. In action Anzio area, 2.–5.44; retreated up Italy; 1.45, inactivated, personnel to Germany.
sPz–Abt.509 With Army Gp.South, 11.43–: in action Proskurov, Kaminets-Podolsk pocket. To Germany 9.44, refitted with King Tigers. To

Hungary 1.45; defensive fighting, until surrendered to US troops Linz, Austria, 5.45.

sPz–Abt.510 On N sector Russian front 8.44–; heavy fighting Kurland; destroyed 8.5.45.

sPz–Abt.511 Partly formed only; some combat in West, '45.

★ ★ ★

Sturmartillerie:

This arm of service was too large and diffuse, and its records are too fragmentary, for more than brief notes on main theatres of deployment of some units:

March 1943: Assault Artillery crewmen, most of them dressed in the early mouse grey/white reversible padded winter combat fatigues, re-ammunition their StuG III Ausf.G assault gun. The loader wears a cloth-and-fleece winter cap, the other field grey Feldmütze with scarves wrapped round them. Interestingly, the Obergefreiter in the background still wears skulls on his field grey, red-piped collar patches even at this date.

France 1940: StuG-Batterie 640, 659, 660, 665; StuG-Abteilung 191

Balkans 1941: StuG-Abt.184, 190, 191

N.Russia, '41–'42: Abt.184, 185; Batt.659—L. Ilmen, Demjansk; Batt.660, 665, 666—form Abt.600, '42; Batt.667—forms Abt.667, '42, to central front. *Central Russia* Abt.191, 244—Kiev; Abt.177, 201, 210, 226—Moscow; Abt.202—with Marders, '42, anti-partisan ops.; Abt.189, 192, 209, 243. *S.Russia* Abt.190, 197, 249—to Crimea, Sevastopol; Abt.244.

Russia, '42–'43: North: Batt.741, 742, Abt.226, Brig.184, 192. *Central, S.Russia:* Abt.190—Stalingrad, survived, then to Kursk. Abt.177, 243, 244, 245—all lost, Stalingrad. Abt.191, 203—Rostov; Brig.232—on Donetz; Abt.(Brig.)667, 189. Abt. 270, Brig.185, 202, 237, 244 (re-formed), 904, 909, 911—all at Kursk. Abt.(Brig.) 191, 209, 243, 259, 276, 279—all in South. Batt.287, Brig.210—

Caucasus: Brig.277, 278—Krivoi Rog. Abt.197—Voronezh, then withdrawn Germany, recd. 'Elefant', 1.43, became Pz.Jäg.Abt.653. (Brig.236—in South; part to Tunisia as 'Batt.Afrika'. Batt.247—to Sardinia, Corsica, '43, anti-partisan ops. with Waffen-SS.)

E.Front, '44–'45; North: Brig.393, 912—Kurland; Brig. 202—Tcherkassy, then Kurland; Brig. 184, 185, 226; 276—Danzig. *Centre, South:* Brig.177 (re-formed), 190, 209, 277, 904, 909—all overrun in East. Brig.249—Berlin. Brig.239—Korsun, Rumania, Budapest. Brig.236, 325—Rumania; Brig.278, 286—Carpathians, Hungary; Brig.301—Brody-Tarnow. Brigs.191, 259, 279, 311, 322, 911—all overrun in East; Brig.210, 237, 394, 667 reached US captivity; Brig.244 trsfd. to West—Arnhem. StuG-Lehr-Brig.I, II, III—Oder, Posen, Berlin.

Western Front Brig.243—Ardennes, Berlin; Brig. 244—Ardennes, Ruhr; Brig.341, 394—Normandy, Ardennes; Brig.911—Ardennes. Brig.914—Italy.

Tank and Armoured Car Uniforms

The Black Vehicle Uniform

The armoured troops of most armies of the 1930s were issued with protective jackets and/or overalls for wear over their normal field service dress when working on, or operating in, their AFVs. The order of 17 November 1934 which established the 'special uniform for German armoured troops'—*Sonderbekleidung der Deutschen Panzertruppen*—was unique in that it introduced a uniform specifically for use in the vehicle, the normal field grey uniform being worn at all other times. Only AFV crews and replacement crews were supposed to be issued with this uniform, all other personnel of armoured regiments retaining the field grey. It should be said at the outset that neither of these two restrictions remained in effective force for very long after the outbreak of war. The prestige of the new Panzer arm, enhanced by its lightning victories in 1939–41, combined with the soldiers' very natural pride in a handsome uniform strikingly different from those worn by all other categories of troops, led to the wearing of the black vehicle uniform almost to the exclusion of the field grey uniform when in the war zone, on duty inside Germany, and—forbidden or not!—on leave or walking out. There was also a steady increase in its use by non-crew personnel of tank regiments and other armoured units.

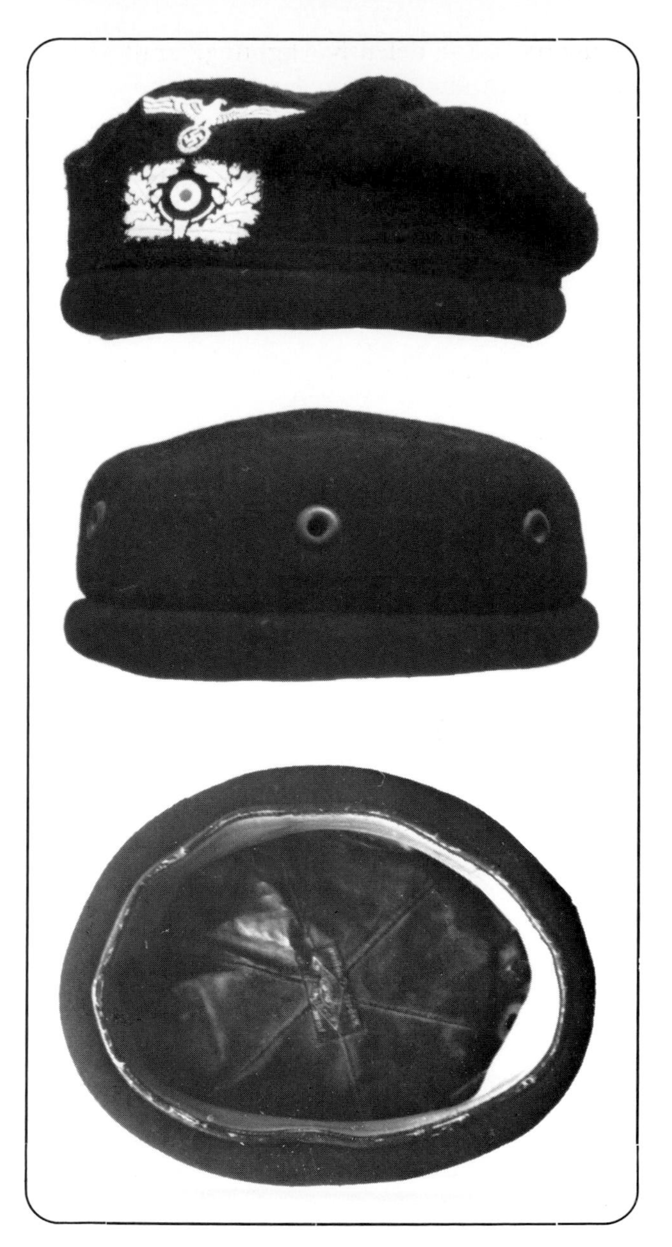

Three views of the Schutzmütze. (Top) the two parts assembled—note prominent padded rim of protective cap showing below edge of 'beret'. (Centre) The padded protective cap with the 'beret' removed; and (Bottom) the interior of the cap, showing oilcloth lining. (Courtesy the late Mike Ross)

The design of the uniform has been attributed to several different influences, all of which probably had a part to play. It was intended to be a practical outfit for men who had to enter, operate in, and leave (sometimes rapidly) the confined space of a tank, crammed with inconveniently placed and potentially dangerous pieces of metal—a tank inevitably oily, dirty and more or less draughty. The uniform was therefore made with a short, tight-fitting jacket without external features which would easily 'snag'; with trousers gathered at the ankle, for the same reason; in a practical black, to conceal stains; and warmly double-breasted. General Guderian himself had a hand in the design, and supposedly copied some of the practical features from ski-clothing.

The headgear was the *Schutzmütze*, a large floppy black beret which fitted over an inner, padded cap of felt and oil-cloth also covered with black wool cloth. The double-breasted cut of the jacket—*Feldjacke*—exposed the shirt, so Panzer personnel were issued a shirt in 'mouse grey' and a black tie.

The jacket was hip-length, with a deep fall collar and broad lapels; the left front fastened over the right almost to the full width of the front torso, the front edge then slanting back towards the centre of the body as it fell to the hem. The fly

Beautiful example of an officer's privately tailored Feldjacke, with the shoulder straps of an Oberstleutnant. There are no buttonholes in the lapels, but the length of ribbon—Eastern Front Winter 1941–42 Medal—is sewn in the appropriate position. The slanting front closure is clearly seen here; the tilted appearance of the breast eagle is due to the jacket being laid flat. (This, and the other two views of this jacket, courtesy Ken Green.)

Left breast lining of the same jacket, showing the size stamping, the pocket, the tightening-tapes at the waist, and the flap for mounting belt-hooks. Note the two small buttons at the edge of the right-hand panel, and the two tape loops on the left-hand lining. The lining in this case is of a light grey drab material.

front concealed a row of large black horn or plastic buttons up the right side of the chest apart from two which were placed above the edge of the lapel as normally worn; these are usually seen in photos immediately above and below the national eagle badge on the right breast. Another button was occasionally placed just under the top inner corner of the right-hand lapel. Three buttonholes spaced along the left lapel corresponded with these buttons, so that in cold weather the lapels could be turned up and across, the jacket then buttoning to the throat. A hook and eye were normally placed at the inner ends of the deep V-notches between collar and lapel on each side, to further secure the neck when the jacket was worn in this way. Some photos in fact show the exposed two buttons removed in the interests of *chic*. Many officers' privately tailored jackets lack them, and in these jackets slight variations to the cut of collar and lapels often make it impossible for the lapels to be buttoned to the top in any case.

One source has stated that Army—as opposed to the slightly different Waffen-SS—jackets had only three buttons on the lower right chest. I have handled several examples with four buttons; it seems unlikely that such details were invariably uniform. Two smaller buttons of the same type were placed on the edge of the right-hand front panel, corresponding with tape loops on the lining of the left front panel, in order to keep the right panel from folding or creasing back on itself when the jacket was fastened. The rear sleeve seam was

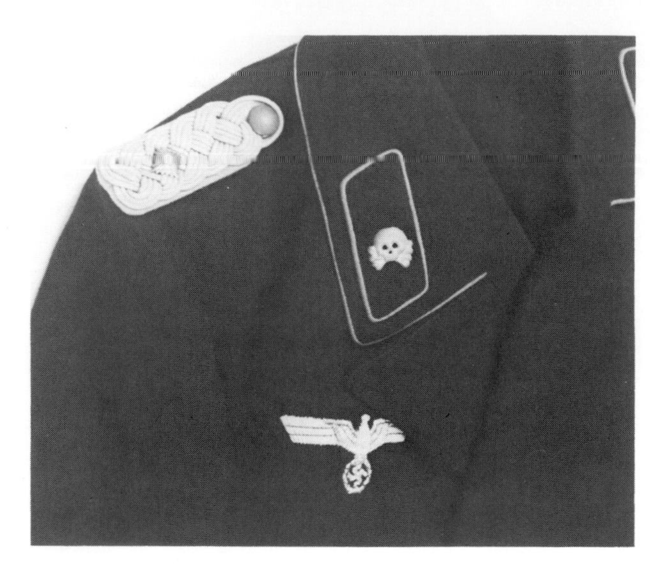

Detail of the Oberstleutnant's shoulder strap, in oxidised-silver finish metallic cord on a pink Waffenfarbe backing, with gold rank 'pip'; the pink collar and collar-patch piping, with oxidised-silver finish pin-on skull; and the officer's breast eagle in heavy silver wire on black backing. Note that the tailoring of this jacket makes it impossible for the lapels to be fastened across and the collar closed; there is no hook-and-eye, and the two small black buttons found above and below the breast eagle on the regulation garment are missing.

split up some 15cm from the cuff, fastening with a fly-button at the wrist. The jacket had a partial lining of drab light grey cotton inside each front panel—see accompanying photo. A pocket was built into the lining of the left panel, and sometimes into both. Tapes passed around the inside of each side of the waistline in cloth 'tunnels', presumably being tied before the jacket was buttoned to improve the fit. Narrow vertical pieces of lining cloth were sewn inside each side seam, with hanging flaps of the same material; these were intended for mounting, at four optional points, belt-support hooks to pass through slits in the side seam, but some of the few examples I have handled have these slits permanently sewn closed. The torso of the jacket was made in four panels,

The special white collar piping and patches of the Luftwaffe's Panzer-Regiment 'Hermann Göring' might seem to disqualify this jacket from consideration in this book; but apart from these applied features its cut and materials are in all respects identical to the Army pattern. Note the details of the right breast lining; here the tab for the belt-hooks is turned up to show inside detail. The lining material in this case is a light grey herringbone twill.

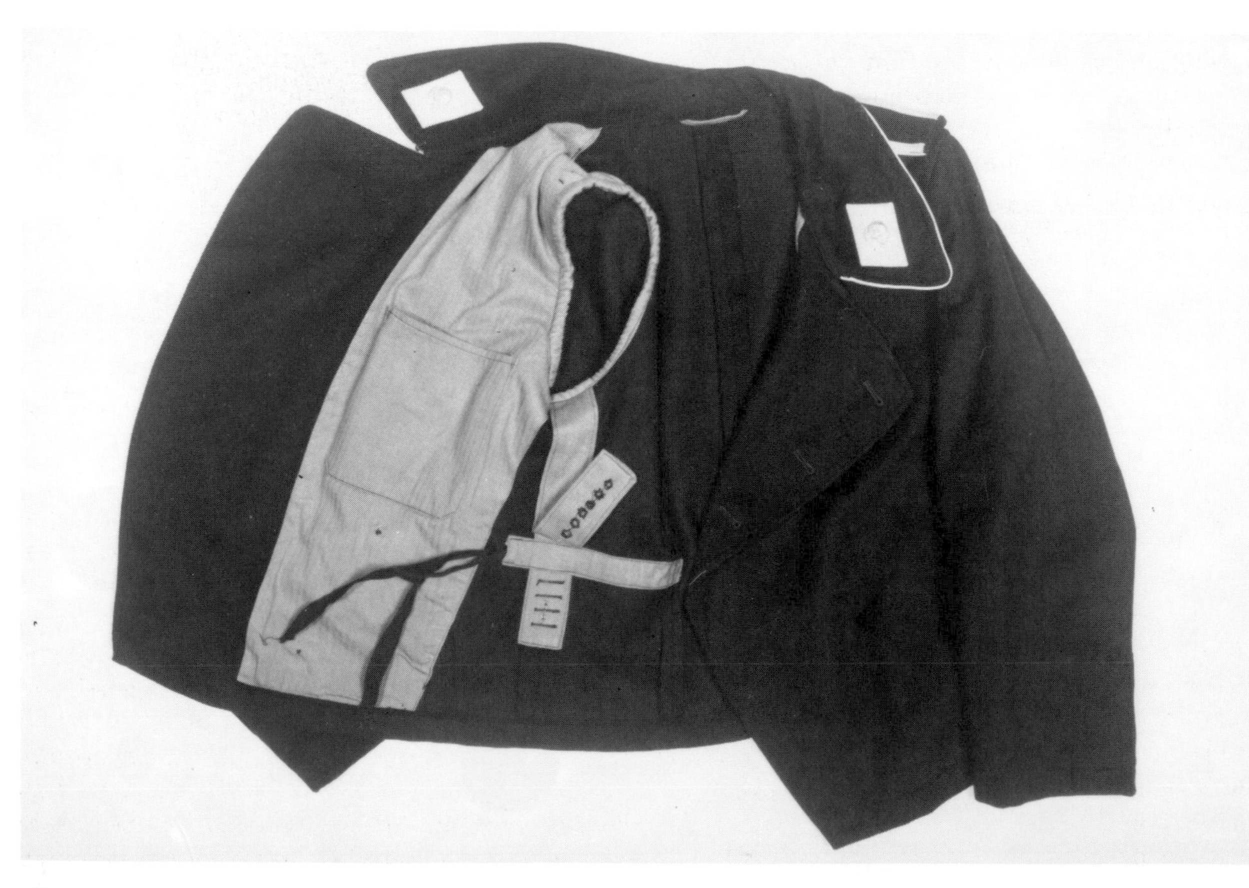

with seams up the sides beneath the arms and a rear central seam. Shorter vertical 'tucks' near the outside edges of the front panels and between the side and rear seams adjusted the fit.

The *Feldhose* were also of black cloth, usually with an integral belt of grey web material exposed at the front of the waist and fastened with a small three-claw metal buckle. Some examples lack this, and have black external belt-loops. There were two slanted side pockets with flaps cut in three shallow points which buttoned forward and downward; a press-stud sometimes replaced the buttons. A small 'fob pocket' was set in the front of the right groin; and one or two horizontally-set rear hip pockets had buttoned or snap-fastened flaps. The legs were cut wide and almost straight to just above the ankle, where they tapered inwards sharply; at the bottom a short split in the outer seam was closed by a button, and tightening-tapes passed through the cloth, allowing the ankle to be fastened tightly. Normally the trousers were worn with the standard German Army high leather marching boot, being gathered *over* the boot so as to give a deep 'bloused' or 'pull-down' effect. Drawings showing examples with tapes for passing under the foot—and thus inside the boot—are therefore rather puzzling; perhaps it was originally intended that they should be worn tucked in, but few if any photos show them worn in this way.

Insignia worn on this uniform were in some respects unique. The edge of the collar was piped in arm-of-service colour, *Waffenfarbe*, for all ranks from private to general: for tank troops, in rose pink. The collars of all ranks bore elongated patches of black cloth in a rhomboid shape, piped pink round the edges, with pinned-on metal death's-head insignia in oxidised silver finish. (The black uniform and silver skull badge invite immediate comparison with the traditional uniform of the 7th or 'Black' Hussars of Frederick the Great's army, and with the later regiments of Prussian Leibhusaren and Brunswick hussars.) The silver *Tresse* or braid worn round the tunic collar of the field grey service uniform by NCOs from Unteroffizier upwards was not worn on the black vehicle uniform. The only ranking was worn on the shoulder straps, and on the upper left sleeve by ranks below Unteroffizier.

The black Panzer trousers, in this case a pair with two rear hip pockets. Note sharply stepped taper at front of ankle and smoother taper at rear, giving the characteristic 'pull-down' shape of these trousers.

The shoulder straps were of the usual German Army design, piped around the edges (apart from the short 'butt end') in arm-of-service colour, and bearing, for Unteroffizier and above, the usual sequence of *Tresse* and silver metal pips. They were of black cloth for all non-commissioned ranks, and fastened with hidden cloth loops and with two silver-grey metal buttons in the normal manner. These buttons, which in pre-war days usually bore an Arabic company number, were the only visible buttons apart from the two high on the chest. The straps were sometimes sewn down to the jacket all round, to prevent 'snagging' in the tank. Officers wore standard shoulder straps of rank in oxidised silver cord on *Waffenfarbe* backing, with gold metal pips as appropriate. Until 1940 regimental numbers were normally worn on the shoulder straps. Ranks below Unteroffizier had them embroidered on the black cloth in *Waffenfarbe*; NCOs wore them in silver metal pin form, and officers in gold metal. This was felt to be inconvenient, and poor security, as the war progressed, and numbers were not worn permanently in the war zones from then on. Metal cyphers could be attached or removed at will, but for enlisted ranks the straps were made blank and cyphers, if required, were added in embroidered form on black slip-over loops.

Ranking in the form of silver-grey chevrons on black backing was worn on the upper left sleeve by the ranks of Gefreiter (one chevron), Obergefreiter (two), Obergefreiter with six years' service (one, with central pip), and Stabsgefreiter (two, with central pip). In 1942 the two-chevrons-and-pip insignia was taken over by the Obergefreiter with six years' service. A single pip worn in the same position was the insignia of the lowest grade, Oberschütze or 'private first class'.

The German Army national eagle and swastika badge was worn on the right breast by all ranks. For enlisted ranks it was initially in white, later in silver-grey or a drabber 'mouse grey'; for officers it was usually in heavy hand-embroidered aluminium wire.

General officers did not normally wear their collar patches of rank on the vehicle uniform, but see Plate F2. Their gold-and-silver-on-red shoulder straps were attached in the normal way, and they wore gold breast eagles. Red striping was not added to the black *Feldhose* for generals.

The insignia worn on the *Schutzmütze* was machine-woven in silver-grey on black cloth backing. It consisted of the oak-wreath enclosing the national cockade, as found on the band of the Army peaked service caps, below a national eagle of normal Army shape. (It should be noted that prior to May 1936 the eagle was not worn on either cap or jacket, being added by an order of 6.5.36.)

Apart from tank crews, certain other types of troops serving in armoured cars or half-tracks were issued the black vehicle uniform with their own distinctions. Pre-war the most important of these were the armoured reconnaissance units, largely formed from cavalry regiments. These wore the black uniform with golden yellow *Waffenfarbe* replacing the pink at all points, and with a Gothic 'A' cypher above the unit number on the shoulder strap. From September 1939 new orders extended the number of different arm-of-service colours which might be seen in the positions described above on the black uniform. The reconnaissance units were expanded beyond the level which could be achieved by drawing them directly from the traditional cavalry regiments. These latter kept their golden yellow *Waffenfarbe*, but armoured car and half-track crews of the new motorised reconnaissance units wore copper-brown. The signals branch *Waffenfarbe* of lemon yellow was applied to the vehicle uniforms of armoured signals personnel in the HQ elements of the Panzer divisions.

Wartime Changes to the Black Vehicle Uniform

The padded beret-style *Schutzmütze* proved unpopular on active service. One reason was the increased fitting of intercom radio in PzKpfw III and IV tanks, which made more widespread the irritation already felt by tank commanders and radio operators at the inconvenience and discomfort of wearing the *Schutzmütze* with the standard radio headset, with its large rubber ear-pads. Officers were able to avoid this by acquiring black versions of the 1938 officer's *Feldmütze*, a sidecap with silver insignia and piping; this is seen in some photos of the September 1939 Polish campaign. By the campaign in the West in May 1940 many enlisted men were wearing the field grey *Feldmütze* of their service uniforms with the black Panzer outfit. This cap had a mouse grey national eagle on a greenish field grey backing sewn to the crown, and the national cockade worked on greenish field grey backing cut in a diamond shape and sewn to the 'turn-up' or band. This latter was enclosed by an inverted V-shape of pink *Waffenfarbe* piping. Photos of the Battle of France show the black officer's sidecap, the grey enlisted man's sidecap and the black beret in simultaneous use.

The issue of a black version of the *Feldmütze* to enlisted ranks was ordered on 27.3.40; this had white or mouse grey national insignia on black backing, and the *Waffenfarbe* piping. Its issue was undertaken in 1940–41 and was almost complete by the Balkan and Russian campaigns of 1941; but in that year photos still show the use of mixed headgear, including the old beret. This was not finally ordered out of use—interestingly, specifically excepting units equipped with the Czech-built PzKpfw 38(t) tank—until January 1941. Steel helmets were issued to AFV crews as standard equipment from March 1941, and they were expected to wear these for protection when crossing rough ground; few did, apart from the tank commander exposed in the cupola when under direct fire—the headset had been impractical to wear with the beret, but with the helmet it was virtually impossible. General issue of helmets ceased in November 1943.

May 1940 saw the Panzer-Pioniere—armoured combat engineers—ordered into the black vehicle uniform, with mixed black/white twist piping at the usual positions. This was worn for about a year, and then this arm of service was ordered to change to the field grey version of the vehicle uniform (see below). Since this allowed the official pioneer *Waffenfarbe*, black, to be seen clearly, the striking black/white piping was discontinued.

Early in 1941 the issue of full-length marching boots to AFV crews was ordered discontinued; a laced ankle-boot and canvas anklet gaiters were to be used instead. The marching boots were retained by those who had them far into the later war years, and nobody seems to have bothered with the anklet, which was unnecessary when the trousers themselves could be gathered and fastened.

Mid-1942 saw the discontinuation of the pink collar piping on the *Feldjacke*, and of the pink *soutache* round the cockade of the *Feldmütze*. This latter order coincided with the issue of the 1942 model of that headgear, which had a turn-up flap split at the front and fastened by two buttons; the cockade moved up to the front of the crown under the eagle, and there was no convenient place for the *soutache*. It should be remembered that the original form of sidecap continued to be worn by those who had it, and in fact the buttoned variety is very rare in wartime photos. Collar piping was also to be seen until the end of the war in photos of veterans, and of officers who chose to keep it as a feature of their privately purchased uniforms.

Fine study of an Unteroffizier tank commander wearing regulation headset and throat microphones; black Feldmütze; and early pattern jacket, with piped collar. The silver Tresse of rank is worn on the shoulder straps inside the line of pink arm-of-service piping; and the original print shows the button to bear an Arabic company number—'8' in this case. The ribbons of the Iron Cross 2nd Class and the Czechoslovak Medal with Prague Bar are pinned to the breast, and below them the Iron Cross 1st Class and the silver Tank Battle Badge. (ECPA)

In March 1943 new *Waffenfarbe* shades were ordered for some types of troops. Armoured car crews of reconnaissance units were now to exchange their copper brown for pink, with an 'A' cypher restored to the shoulder straps; armoured train personnel were also to wear pink with an 'E' cypher. Units traditionally linked with cavalry regiments seem to have retained golden yellow piping.

From mid-1943 the black sidecap was progressively replaced with a black version of the *Einheitsfeldmütze*, the 'ski-cap' type of headgear

Rare photographic evidence for the wearing of black-and-white twist piping on the collar, collar patches and shoulder straps of Panzer-Pioniere in 1940–41. This Hauptfeldwebel, photographed in Russia in summer 1941, wears a Wound Badge on the left breast. (Bundesarchiv)

August 1943: Major Dr. Franz Bäke, second from left (see also Plate H1), at that time serving with Pz-Regt.11, 6.Pz-Div., photographed with brother officers. Note details of early mouse grey shirt, without pockets or shoulder strap attachments and worn without insignia apart from the Knight's Cross at the throat.

which was increasingly to replace the sidecap in all branches of the German forces. This had a split turn-up with two buttons, the usual eagle and cockade being worn above it on the crown. Officers had a version piped silver at the crown seam, and not uncommonly had unauthorised silver piping in the front scallop of the turn-up as well. Again, the previous pattern was very widely retained right up to the end of the war.

The mouse grey shirt, as originally issued, had no pockets or shoulder straps, and no insignia or decorations (other than the Knight's Cross at the throat) were worn with it. A later version, apparently produced both in mouse grey and field grey, had pleated breast pockets with buttoned flaps, and attachments for shoulder straps; it was often seen with the breast eagle, and indeed with decorations and war badges. In mid-1943 a dark grey shirt was introduced for Panzer personnel, with pockets and shoulder strap attachments. Photos show shirts of all shades of grey, as well as privately acquired black shirts. A popular alternative was a roll-neck sweater, usually grey but sometimes black.

From about 1944 armoured personnel were not normally issued with the field grey service uniform, wearing their black uniform for all duties; this did not apply to officers, however.

Officers' Headgear

While not actually part of the prescribed vehicle uniform, two types of headgear were so universally worn by Panzer officers as to require mention under this heading. These were the standard officers peaked service cap—*Schirmmütze*—and the 'old style officer's field cap. Both were of field grey with a dark green band, and were piped in *Waffenfarbe* at crown seam and both band edges. The *Schirmmütze* had a wire stiffener in the crown (often removed in the front line), a stiff peak of black patent fibre, and two silver chin-cords. On the front of the crown was worn a national eagle, either in silver metal or in silver wire embroidery on dark green cloth. The band bore a silver oak-wreath surrounding the national cockade; again, both metal and silver wire embroidered versions were seen. The 'old style field cap' for officers was supposed to have been replaced by the sidecap style in 1938, and was again specifically discontinued by an order of 1942; it was so popular, however, that it was still to be seen in 1945. Basically similar to the *Schirmmütze* but of smaller outline, it had no crown stiffener or cords; the peak was of semi-flexible leather, and the insignia were machine-woven, flat, on green cloth patches.

Denims and Protective Clothing

The black uniform was often covered—or replaced, in hot weather—by working denims of a wide variety of styles. The earliest issue was the old pre-war 'drill uniform', its original off-white dyed green. This consisted of a shapeless jacket with a small fall collar, five field grey front buttons, and two patch or slit skirt pockets, worn with straight, loose trousers. By 1941 significant numbers of one-piece denim suits from Czech stocks were being issued. Of a light neutral khaki/stone colour, these were baggy 'boiler-suits' with a broad fall collar, slit side pockets in the trouser part, and usually, but not invariably, two flapped breast pockets. Photos show Panzer collar patches, shoulder straps and breast eagles applied to these suits. These and other types of denim overalls sometimes seem to have been dyed black for wear by mechanics, in which case insignia were rare.

Well-known but classic study of a young Leutnant tank commander in 1944, wearing the 'old style officer's field cap'—popular for its small size and unstiffened shape, allowing it to be worn conveniently with a headset.

Photographed in 1942, this junior officer appears to be wearing the green denim fatigue and summer uniform introduced for the Army as a whole in that year.

In May 1941 a green drill version of the black vehicle uniform was introduced for armoured car crews; it was cut identically to the black uniform, and worn both as a working denim and as summer combat dress. It bore a mouse grey national eagle, and initially conventional ranking was worn in the form of the shoulder straps from the field grey

Panzer crewman prowling outside his tank, armed with the MP.40 carried in clips inside the turret of most AFVs. The jacket collar is folded outside a denim overall which appears to be the Czech-made type used in some numbers in the early war years.

uniform and sleeve chevrons on a field grey or reed green backing. In August 1942 it was ordered that these marks of rank be replaced by the new system of green-on-black bars and oak-sprays introduced that month for wear on clothing without shoulder straps (see F5, H3). Tank crews also acquired quantities of these armoured car denims.

In 1942 a 'universal' denim uniform was introduced for the Army as a whole. This was a version, in reed green cotton, of the field grey service dress, and resembled it in most details. The four pockets of the tunic were unpleated and had straight-cut flaps in most cases, but photos also show examples with box pleats and pointed flaps. The national eagle was worn on the right breast in mouse grey, and the normal field service quality collar bars—*Litzen*—on the collar. The trousers had buttoned slit side pockets without flaps, and a small flapped fob pocket in the right groin; there were attachments for braces, and two belt loops at the front. The legs were cut straight, and had a buttoning tab at the bottom. This outfit was frequently worn by Panzer crews in the absence of special armoured-pattern denims.

In the same year a special reed green denim outfit specifically for tank-crews was introduced. Of basically the same cut as the black uniform, it was made looser in the torso, with two parallel rows of buttons on the right panel; these allowed it to be worn either over or instead of the black uniform and to be buttoned neatly in both cases. Its main distinguishing feature was a large external flapped pocket on the left chest, and another on the front of the left thigh, the former sometimes set at a slight slant from the vertical; these allow photos of this outfit to be distinguished from the armoured car denims. Collar patches were often applied, as were trade badges, and sometimes battle badges and decorations. Shoulder straps were not normally worn, but are sometimes seen attached; the official ranking method was the system of green-on-black patches worn on the left upper sleeve.

Before the winter of 1942–43 the only extra winter clothing available to tank crews was the standard field grey greatcoat. This had a deep fall collar faced dark green, and two rows of six buttons on the double-breasted front. In the winter of 1941–42 tank men, like every other German in Russia, adopted every kind of improvisation in order to stay alive, and weird concoctions of fur, leather, cloth, wool and straw are to be seen in photos. By the following winter the excellent padded, reversible German Army winter combat suit was available. This had at first one side in mouse grey and one side in white; the grey was later changed to the Army camouflage scheme of 'splinter', and later still of 'water' pattern. The long double-breasted jacket had a hood attached, a fastening fly offset to the right with metal buttons, two skirt pockets, drawstrings at waist and hem, and adjustable cuffs. The over-trousers were cut rather short and could be worn either inside or outside the boots, drawstringed at the ankle. The left sleeve rank-patch system was used on this outfit.

1. Bandsman, Pz-Regt.5, 1935
2. Feldwebel Fahnenträger, Pz-Regt.5, 1939
3. Hauptmann, Pz-Regt.5, parade dress, 1939

A

1. Oberwachtmeister, Pz-Regt.24; Russia, 1942
2. Obergefreiter, Panzertruppe; Russia, 1941
3. Gefreiter, Aufklärungstruppe; Russia, 1942

B

1. Unteroffizier, StuG-Abt.192; Russia, 1941
2. Oberwachtmeister, StuG-Abt.202; Russia, 1942-43
3. Feldwebel,Pz-Jgd-Abt.,Pz-Regt. 'Kurmark'; Russia, 1945

C

1. Oberfeldwebel, Aufkl-Abt.33; Libya, 1941
2. Feldwebel, Pz-Regt.8; Libya, 1941-42
3. Oberleutnant, Pz-Regt.8; Libya, 1942

D

1. Panzerschütze, sPz-Abt.503; Normandy, 1944
2. Schütze, Pz-Aufkl-Abt.115; Italy, summer 1944
3. Panzerschütze, Normandy, 1944

E

1. Oberst Graf Strachwitz, Pz-Regt.'GD';1943
2. Generalmajor Schultz, 7.Pz-Div.; 1944
3. Oberst, Panzertruppe; Italy,1944
4. Oberst Schmidt, sPz-Abt.507; 1944
5. Major, Pz-Regt.16; 1944

F

1. Gefreiter, Sturmartillerie; 1941
2. Major, Aufkl-Abt.33; 1944
3. Leutnant, StuG-Bde.276; 1944
4. Major, StuG-Abt.249; 1944-45
5. Hauptmann, Sturmartillerie; 1945

G

1. Major Dr.Franz Bäke, 1943-44
2. Generalmajor Mäder, 'F-G-Div.'; 1944-45
3. Major Jähde, sPz-Abt.502; 1944
1
2
3

H

Tropical Uniforms

These are illustrated and described in the colour plates, commentaries and photo captions. Panzer personnel wore exactly the same tropical uniforms and insignia as all other German Army personnel in the desert. The use of the skulls from the vehicle uniform collar patches, and of the tropical sidecap, is illustrated on Plate D.

Panther crew of Pz-Lehr-Regt.130 photographed in Hungary early in 1944 wearing the camouflaged, reversible, padded winter combat fatigue suit. (ECPA)

Self-Propelled Artillery Uniforms

Before approaching this complex subject a definition of terms is necessary.

German self-propelled artillery equipments of many kinds, in enclosed armoured or open-topped mountings on tank chassis, served with a number of different kinds of unit. The Assault Gun Battalions, later renamed Assault Gun Brigades and later still Assault Artillery Brigades (Sturmgeschütz-Abteilung, – Brigade; Sturmartillerie-Brigade) formed a distinct arm of service. Equipped with the various marks of StuG III, StuG IV and StuH 42 assault guns, they were intended to act as close-support units for the infantry; it was an essential feature of the new style of armoured warfare that the battle tank would not generally be available for this rôle. These assault gun units sometimes served within Panzer and Panzer-Grenadier divisions, but more commonly came under Corps or Army command and were allocated according to temporary necessity. Assault guns also served as part of the support units within infantry and Panzer-Grenadier regiments in the second half of the war.

Self-propelled anti-tank guns—Panzerjäger, Jagdpanzer—were not available in significant numbers until 1941–42. They were of a bewildering variety of types, many of them cobbled together by marrying German or captured Russian and French artillery pieces with the chassis of obsolescent German, Czech and French tanks. The most prominent were the several marks of Marder, and the fine purpose-built German 'heavy tank destroyers', the Nashorn and Jagdpanther. They were steadily incorporated from 1941 onwards into the integral anti-tank battalions of infantry, Panzer and Panzer-Grenadier divisions; into the anti-tank companies of infantry and Panzer-Grenadier regiments; and into independent Army and Corps units.

The field artillery regiments of Panzer and Panzer-Grenadier divisions began the war with towed guns, but in 1942–45 a proportion of self-propelled mountings such as the Hummel and Wespe were incorporated.

The basic uniform appeared after trials in May 1940, for wear by crews and replacement crews of Assault Gun units. As originally envisaged it was a field grey version of the black Panzer vehicle uniform, complete with the padded beret. The trials batch had dark green upper collars with *Litzen* collar patches; the issued uniforms were all-over field grey. Collar patches were of Panzer shape, but in field grey piped with artillery-red *Waffenfarbe*, with metal skulls. (One source has stated that the patches were dark green; there may have been some early issue of these, but all photos which I have studied show field grey.) The collar was not piped red, and *Tresse* was not worn on the collar by NCOs. Breast eagles, shoulder straps and all other insignia were as worn on the field grey service uniform. The beret had white or silver-grey insignia on dark green backing, identical in design to those on the black Panzer version. Its issue is something of a puzzle; photos of the first four batteries during the French campaign of 1940 show the field grey *Feldmütze*, and so do photos of the Balkan and Russian campaigns of spring–summer 1941. The beret was

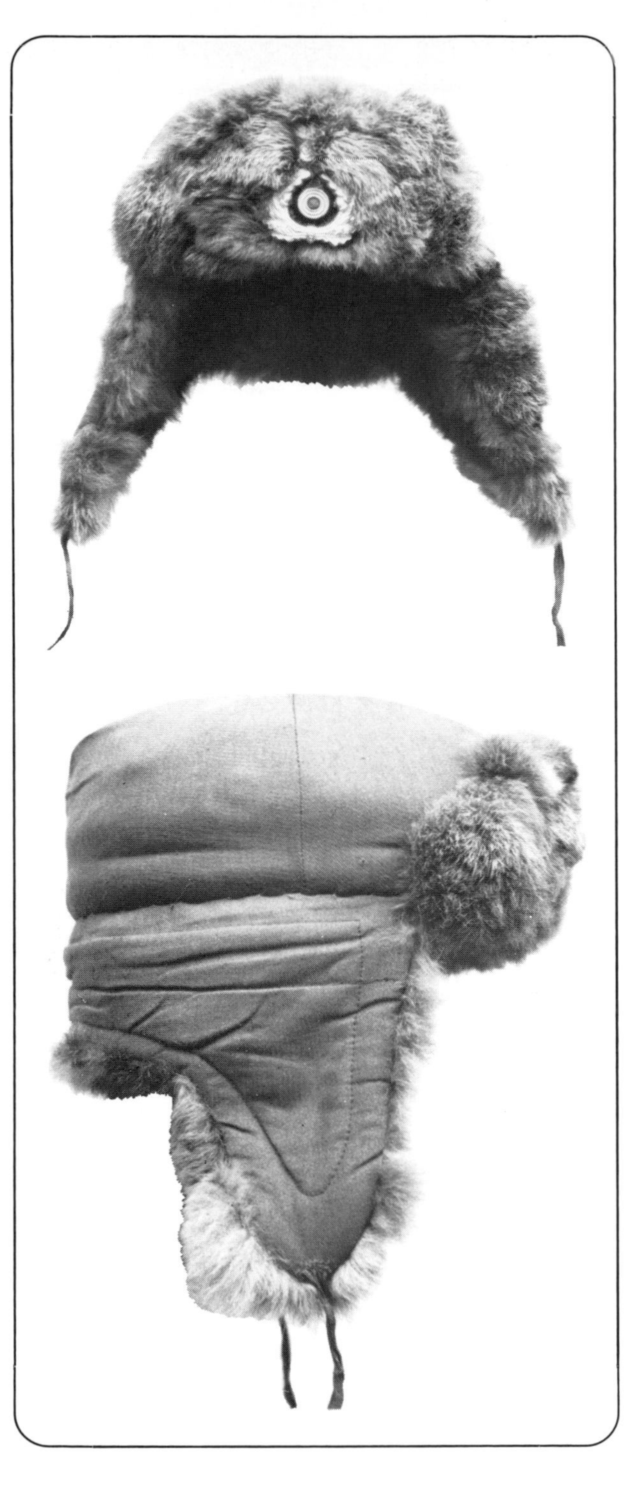

Two views of a winter cap made by the prominent German hatters Erel, apparently by covering the inner padded cap of the discarded Schutzmütze with field grey cloth, and adding ear, neck and front flaps faced with rabbit-fur. In the side view the characteristic rim of the Schutzmütze can be seen. (Courtesy R. Tredwen)

ordered out of use at the same time as the black model in January 1941. Yet a photo clearly shows an NCO of StuG-Abt.192 wearing it in Russia in 1941 (see Plate C1). It was certainly very little worn.

The collar patches worn by Sturmartillerie units are a cause of great confusion, and photos suggest little uniformity between units. Firstly, at some time in 1941, the skulls were ordered removed; photos from the initial Russian invasion show personnel of some units wearing 'empty red boxes' on their collars, but others show the skull retained until at least 1944. One main source suggests that it was in January 1943 that the skull-patches were ordered removed altogether, and replaced by conventional *Litzen*. Officers wore the same *Litzen* as on their service uniforms; enlisted ranks wore them enclosed by red piping, on a backing of green or sewn down to the field grey collar without backing. Supposedly this order held good until the end of the war. In March 1943 assault gunners serving within the support elements of infantry and Panzer-Grenadier regiments were ordered to wear the *Litzen* enclosed with white or green piping respectively; all others retained the red.

So far, so good . . . if it were universally true! But photos show the continued use of field grey patches with and without skulls alongside the red-piped *Litzen*—sometimes within the same unit—until at least mid-1944 in some cases. Worse—photos taken in the last two years of the war show a number of cases of Sturmartillerie officers and men wearing the black Panzer vehicle uniform, with (apparently) pink-piped collars and 'empty' black, pink-piped collar patches, at the same time as field grey headgear and—presumably—shoulder straps with pink *Waffenfarbe*, since a mixture of two different *Waffenfarben* on the same uniform would be extraordinary. Could this come about simply through use of the old pattern of black uniform in cases of shortage of the correct grey version? Several photos show officers of assault artillery brigades wearing a wild mixture of uniforms and insignia, of which one of the most extraordinary is a group from StuG-Bde.276 in East Prussia in November 1944. Of ten unit officers five wear grey and five black vehicle uniforms. To be precise, the photo shows three men in grey with *Litzen* patches; two in grey with patches obscured; three in black with *Litzen* patches; and two in black with Panzer skull patches—whether or not with pink collar piping cannot be made out. Several other photos of 1944–45 show the *Litzen* worn on the black uniform by assault artillery officers of different units. The author confesses himself utterly at a loss to explain these variations.

In the SP anti-tank units—Panzerjäger—the situation is as complex, but at least it appears to have been subject to regulations, even if they were often ignored or were unevenly obeyed. It seems that the first generation of SP anti-tank guns were crewed by men wearing sometimes the black vehicle uniform with pink *Waffenfarbe* and a 'P' shoulder strap cypher, and sometimes the field grey service uniform with the same distinctions. In February 1942 the expanding branch was ordered into the grey vehicle uniform. (Yet I have handled an apparently original field grey vehicle uniform stamped 1941, with 'empty' field grey collar patches showing no signs of ever having borne skulls, outlined in pink. Dark green shoulder straps, piped pink, bore no 'P' cyphers.) They were to retain the black, pink-piped skull patches, and the pink *Waffenfarbe* and cypher on their dark green (later, economy-pattern field grey) shoulder straps. The proliferation of anti-tank equipments in various types of unit apparently caused confusion, because in May 1944 a comprehensive new set of orders appeared. From then on the following distinctions were—officially—observed:

Panzerjäger units within Panzer and Panzer-Grenadier divisions, and Army or Corps units with the 'Elefant' heavy tank destroyer were to wear the black uniform, distinguished from tank crews only by the 'P' cypher.

All other types of Panzerjäger unit under Army or Corps command, or integral to infantry, rifle, and mountain *divisions* were to wear the grey vehicle uniform with the black collar patches, pink *Waffenfarbe* and 'P' cypher.

Panzerjäger units integral to infantry, rifle and mountain *regiments* were to wear grey vehicle uniforms, pink *Waffenfarbe* and 'P' on the shoulder straps, but *Litzen* enclosed in the appropriate piping—i.e. white or green—on the collar.

5 September 1942: Gen. von Salmuth decorates Oblt. Otto Hoffmann of StuG-Abt.201 with the Knight's Cross, which he was awarded on 31 July that year. On Hoffmann's turned-up collar can be seen the original Sturmartillerie patch—field grey, piped artillery red, with applied metal skull—which was supposedly discontinued many months before. For this parade Hoffmann wears a gilt '201' pinned to his shoulder straps.

While able to suggest no comprehensive explanation for the confusing mixture of uniforms and insignia shown by the photos mentioned above of Sturmartillerie personnel in 1944–45, I would suggest that one reason may lie in the serious blurring of function between the Panzer, Panzerjäger and Sturmartillerie units in this period. Self-propelled guns were quicker and cheaper to make than tanks with revolving turrets; and as the war became essentially a defensive struggle for Germany the SP gun—as effective in this rôle as the tank—increasingly usurped the place of the tank on the battlefield. Towards the end of the war many nominally 'Panzer' battalions, in Panzer and Panzer-Grenadier divisions, were in fact equipped with assault guns. The SP guns which had been introduced specifically as infantry support weapons proved effective as tank-killers, and were increasingly used in that rôle by commanders starved of

Hptm. Mangold, commanding the Sturmgeschütz-Abteilung of the 'Grossdeutschland' Division, wearing the grey vehicle uniform. The cords and insignia from a Schirmmütze seem to have been added to an 'old style field cap' in this case. He wears regulation officer's collar Litzen patches; the divisional cuff title; a dark grey shirt; regulation officer's grey suede gloves; and decorations including the cloth version of the War Order of the German Cross below the breast eagle. Note trouser pocket detail, identical to that of the black Panzer trousers. (Bundesarchiv)

battle tanks. The nominal difference in rôle between assault artillery and SP anti-tank artillery became virtually meaningless. In this situation, perhaps some confusion over uniform distinctions is not surprising?

The grey vehicle uniform worn with conventional collar *Litzen* and *Waffenfarbe* of the appropriate arm spread to other types of unit. All personnel of assault artillery and anti-tank units operating armour acquired the uniform. From 1944 this embraced some Panzer-Grenadier units—mechanised infantry—within armoured formations, and also some armoured reconnaissance units. From May 1943 it officially replaced the black uniform of armoured train personnel, with pink *Waffenfarbe* and the 'E' cypher; and was issued to Army anti-aircraft personnel crewing SP mountings, with red *Waffenfarbe*. Its use also spread in those field artillery units which operated the Hummel, Wespe and other SP equipments. These had started their career in the usual field grey service uniform, but increasingly adopted the grey vehicle uniform with red *Waffenfarbe* and collar *Litzen*.

Headgear in SP artillery units of all kinds paralleled that in the Army as a whole. The field grey sidecap was worn until mid-1943, and was then progressively replaced with the field grey *Einheitsfeldmütze*. Denims seem to have been of all the types described for Panzer troops, simply according to availability.

★ ★ ★

Decorations and Battle Badges

Members of armoured units wore the full range of gallantry decorations and wound badges authorised by the German armed forces in exactly the same positions on the vehicle uniforms as on the field grey service uniform. Where ribbons were worn in the tunic buttonhole (e.g. Iron Cross 2nd Class, Iron Cross 1914, Winter 1941–42 Medal, etc.) they were normally worn in the upper buttonhole of the left lapel or sewn to the lapel in the appropriate position where a private-purchase officer's tunic lacked actual buttonholes.

Battle or 'assault' badges appropriate to the armoured branch of the Army were as follows:

Panzerkampfabzeichen Instituted 20.12.39, for award to officers and men of tank crews who had taken part in three armoured attacks on three different days. A silver badge, made in both cast and stamped versions, it was in the form of an oval oak-wreath surmounted by the 'armed forces' folded-wing eagle and swastika, containing a ¾-front presentation of a stylised Panzer. Awarded on the authority of divisional commanders, the badge was intended to replace earlier awards of the Condor Legion tank badge. After June 1943 higher grades were introduced for greater numbers of attacks, with '25', '50', '75' and '100' inset on small rectangular cartouches at the bottom centre of the wreath. The design changed in small details, the Panzer becoming more modern in appearance. The '25' and '50' badges were slightly larger than the basic style, the tank being in black. The '75' and '100' badges were still larger, the wreath being in gilt. At least one example of a '200' badge is known.

From June 1940 a bronze version of the basic badge was awarded to armoured car crews, and to Panzer-Grenadiers and medical personnel who qualified by attacks in armoured personnel carriers. The '25' and '50' badges were also bronze; '75' and '100' badges had bronze tanks on gilt wreaths.

Allsemeines Sturmabzeichen The General Assault Badge, instituted 1.6.40, was awarded to personnel who took part in three attacks on three different days but who did not qualify for the Infantry Assault or Tank Battle badges—i.e. primarily artillery, engineer, anti-tank and anti-aircraft personnel. The silver badge comprised the conventional wreath, containing the 'armed forces' eagle and swastika above a crossed bayonet and stick-grenade. From June 1943 higher grades were awarded, as follows: Grades II and III = '25' and '50' cartouches; larger, black eagles and emblems on silver wreaths. Grade IV = '75' and '100', larger still, gold wreaths. A time qualification was adopted for calculating entitlement: eight months' front-line service = ten attacks, 12 months = 15 attacks, and 15 months = 25 attacks. The General Assault Badge was frequently awarded to self-propelled artillery and anti-tank personnel.

Cuff titles Armoured personnel of several units qualified for the 'Afrikakorps' cuff title, worn on the right forearm by DAK officers and men with at least two months' service in that theatre. Instituted 18.7.41, the dark green cloth band bore the legend 'Afrikakorps' in silver capitals and silver edge-stripes, with brown outer edges.

This was superseded from 15.1.43 by a cuff title worn as a commemorative rather than a formation insignia, and worn by qualified personnel until the end of the war. In light brown cloth, the band had silver-grey edge-piping and the word 'Afrika' in silver-grey capitals between two silver-grey palm-heads. It was worn on the left arm.

Personnel of 2nd Bn., Panzer-Regiment 31 qualified for the Crete invasion cuff title, instituted 16.10.42. A white band with yellow edge-piping bore the word 'Kreta' in yellow capitals between two yellow acanthus-leaf motifs. It was worn on the left arm.

Some armoured personnel presumably received the 'Kurland' title, locally manufactured and issued by Army Group Courland between 12.3.45 and the end of the war. Worn on the left sleeve, the silver-grey or off-white band had black borders with an intermittent black inner border, and the word 'Kurland' in black capitals between the shield of the Grand Master of the Teutonic Knights and the elk-head arms of Mitau, both worked in black on ground colour.

Winter 1943–44: mechanics work on the engine of a StuG III of the StuG-Abt. 'Grossdeutschland'; two different types of winter cap are worn, together with the reversible padded winter fatigues (left) and a one-piece denim overall.

The black vehicle uniform and Schutzmütze worn by crewmen of a self-propelled anti-tank gun (4.7cm PAK(t) on a PzKpfw I chassis) of Pz.Jäg.Abt.521 during the campaign in the West, 1940. On the right ribs the brass hook passing through the jacket to engage with the belt can just be seen.

The Plates

A1: Bandsman, Panzer-Regiment 5, 1935

The *Schutzmütze* and black jacket lack the national eagle badge, introduced for the Panzer uniform in May 1936. On some early berets a small central stalk of material is seen. The regimental number was embroidered on the shoulder strap in pink *Waffenfarbe*. Regimental musicians wore traditional 'swallows' nests' or shoulder wings, in *Waffenfarbe* with braiding, hooked to the jacket shoulder seam. Drummers and fifers had dull grey braid; bandsmen and trumpeters bright silver braid; and battalion buglers, bright silver braid and a 7cm silver fringe at the bottom edge.

A2: Feldwebel Fahnenträger, Panzer-Regiment 5, 1939

The national eagle is now worn on cap and right breast, in silver-grey by this NCO. The regimental number is pinned to his shoulder straps in silver metal; the straps bear silver *Tresse* (braid) and pips of rank as well as branch-colour piping. Parade additions to the black vehicle uniform include the marksmanship lanyard fixed from the right shoulder to the front buttons, one of several grades differing in small details of design; the standard-bearer's gorget worn round the neck; and the carrying-sash for the flag, made of leather faced with silver braid and with silk in the appropriate *Waffenfarbe*. The standard-bearer's elaborate cloth arm-shield insignia, introduced in 1936 for wear on field grey uniforms, was sometimes but not invariably worn on the black jacket. The cavalry-style standards, of a deep rose shade, were awarded one per battalion.

A3: Hauptmann, Panzer-Regiment 5: parade dress, 1939

Panzer officers naturally owned the full range of uniforms required by regulation, including field grey service and uniform tunics, breeches, etc.; but with the increasing prestige of the Panzer arm, and the increased use of the black vehicle uniform for orders of dress not originally authorised, the more mundane field grey service dress was less in evidence than in other branches. The black uniform was worn for parades in the vehicles, with the addition of parade decorations such as, for commissioned ranks, the silver aiguillettes and the silver and dark green belt. For dismounted parades the normal *Paradeanzug für Offiziere* was worn, as illustrated.

The tunic is the ornate 'uniform tunic' or *Waffenrock*, with dark green facings at cuff and collar; *Waffenfarbe* piping; and silver cuff and collar patches on backgrounds of *Waffenfarbe*. The national eagle is in silver on Panzer black, and the shoulder straps of rank are on *Waffenfarbe* backing and bear a gold pinned-on regimental number between the 'pips'. The aiguillettes are purely decorative, signifying nothing more than officer rank; so is the belt, which does not support the steel sword scabbard—this is suspended from internal fixtures under the tunic. The sword-knot is of grey leather striped with silver, the knob or

A roadside briefing for a tired, dusty Panzer troop during the lightning advances of summer 1941. A mixture of black uniform and denim clothing is worn.

tassel of silver braid only. The breeches are of grey rather than field grey; they have no stripe or piping, and are worn with conventional top-boots fitted for parades with strapped spurs. The helmet is neatly painted—many shades of field grey or grey were seen—with the usual Army decals on each side.

The medals on the left breast are for four and twelve years' Army service, and for participation in the Austrian Anschluss. The badge below them is the silver Condor Legion tank personnel badge, whose introduction by von Thoma in 1936 was confirmed by the German Army in July 1939. In June 1939 a cuff title had been authorised for former members of the Condor Legion's tank units, to be worn on the service blouse and uniform tunic but not—sadly!—on the vehicle jacket. It was of red and gold, and bore the legend '1936 Spanien 1939' in Gothic lettering.

B1: Oberwachtmeister ('Spiess'), Panzer-Regiment 24; Russia, 1942

The yellow piping at collar, collar patch, shoulder strap and cap front is the regimental distinction of this unit, formed in 1942 from the old 1st Cavalry Regiment and allowed to retain cavalry piping and traditions. Otherwise the uniform is conventional for a company sergeant-major in 'reporting order', with his 'reporting pouch' tucked into the jacket front in traditional manner. The two silver braid cuff rings identify an appointment, not a rank—the '*Spiess*', or company/squadron sergeant-major. The black *Feldmütze* introduced in 1940 was in universal use by 1942. Decorations are the ribbon of the Winter 1941 Medal in the buttonhole, a black Wound Badge

Oberwachtmeister Richard Schramm of StuG-Bde.202, awarded the Knight's Cross in December 1942 for destroying a total of 44 Soviet AFVs; he was later posted missing, believed killed. See Plate C2. His assault gun seems to be christened 'Sea Devil'.

(one or two wounds), and a silver Panzer Battle Badge.

B2: Panzer Obergefreiter: Russia, 1941

The withdrawal of the *Schutzmütze* and the introduction of the black *Feldmütze* did not coincide, and many photos taken in 1940–41 show the use of the field grey *Feldmütze* as an interim measure. The pre-war denim fatigue uniform of off-white material, hard-wearing but shapeless, was one of several types of working clothing employed by armoured units, dyed various shades of grey or black. It seems to have been popular to wear the trousers as over-trousers, leaving the black jacket exposed. The normal Army sleeve ranking is worn, in silver-grey braid on a black backing triangle. This veteran of the 1940 campaign wears the ribbon of the Iron Cross 2nd Class in his lapel buttonhole, and the silver Panzer Battle Badge pinned to the left breast.

B3: Gefreiter, Aufklärungs unit; Russia, 1942

Of the same cut as the black vehicle uniform but in a lightweight green duck material, the combat and working uniform illustrated was introduced from May 1941 for use by armoured car crews in reconnaissance units; it was later seen in use by some tank crews as working or hot-weather uniform. The national eagle is in 'mouse-grey' on a greenish backing, and the chevron of rank in dull grey braid on field grey. The shoulder straps from the field grey service uniform are added, in the 'economy' version seen increasingly from 1942, of field grey rather than dark green cloth. The piping is copper-brown; the reconnaissance units changed to pink *Waffenfarbe* with an 'A' cypher from March 1943. Above the chevron is the qualification badge of a signaller in a non-signals unit: the 'blitz' in branch colour on a dark green oval. Other trade badges were worn on the right forearm, usually in yellow on dark green or field grey discs irrespective of branch. On the left chest is the bronze version of the Panzer Battle Badge authorised for armoured car personnel and Panzer-Grenadiers of units equipped with armoured vehicles. The normal crew sidearm was the Walther P.38 pistol holstered on the left hip. The MP.40 sub-machine gun was also carried in most armoured vehicles for crew use.

C1: Unteroffizier, Sturmgeschütz-Abteilung 192; Russia, 1941

The field grey version of the tank uniform was approved after trials in May 1940. The few Assault Gun Batteries which served in the West in 1940 seem from photos to have worn a mixture of this uniform and the conventional German Army field grey service dress, with field grey *Feldmützen* and steel helmets but not, apparently, the field grey *Schutzmütze*. The black and grey versions of this headgear were ordered out of use in January 1941; nevertheless, a photo certainly shows at least one in use, by an NCO of this unit in Russia in summer 1941. The uniform is generally similar to the black version. The collar patches are field grey, piped artillery red, with applied metal skulls. The dark green shoulder straps are those of the conventional service uniform, with silver *Tresse* of rank and red branch piping. A Wound Badge and a General Assault Badge are worn on the left chest. The headset and throat microphones are those worn by commanders and wireless operators of all armoured vehicles for most of the war; the inconvenience of wearing the headset over the *Schutzmütze* is shown here.

C2: Oberwachtmeister, Sturmgeschütz-Abteilung 202; Russia, 1942–43

Cavalry ranks were retained in tactical units formed from parent regiments of the traditional mounted branches, including some assault artillery units. The field grey *Feldmütze* has a V of artillery red *soutache* piping and conventional national insignia. The collar patches are the conventional field service quality *Litzen*, silver-grey bars on a greenish field grey backing, worn in this branch with red outline piping. (Typical of the complexity of this subject is the fact that the *Ritterkreuzträger* on whom this painting is based, Richard Schramm, is seen in two photos taken within weeks of one another wearing both these patches, and the old field grey 'skull' patches piped red.) Shoulder straps of 'economy' pattern bear, apart from normal ranking, the two silver loops identifying an *Offizieranwärter* or officer aspirant. The Knight's Cross was always worn at the throat; the Iron Cross 1st Class pinned to the chest; and the ribbon of the Iron Cross 2nd Class either in the buttonhole, or on a ribbon bar on the left breast. A silver Wound Badge (three or four wounds) and the General Assault Badge are also worn here.

C3: Feldwebel, I (Pz.Jgd.) Abteiling, Panzer-Regiment 'Kurmark'; Eastern Front, 1945

This NCO, based on a photo of the *Ritterkreuzträger* Fw.Riedmüller, shows regulation *Panzerjäger* uniform and insignia. The field grey 1943 *Einheitsfeldmütze* bears a personal affectation, the metal national eagle from a *Schirmmütze* pinned to the crown above the cockade. The field grey SP artillery uniform has the black and pink 'skull' patches of Panzer troops; and the shoulder straps in dark green, piped pink, bear the 'P' of SP anti-tank units in silver metal.

D1: Oberfeldwebel, Aufklärungs-Abteilung 33; Libya, 1941

The rather cumbersome sun helmet issued to the DAK on its arrival in Africa was unpopular, and soon gave way to the peaked tropical field cap and the steel helmet. However, the capture of stocks of the much smaller and handier South African Army sun helmet led to its widespread use by German troops, who pinned to its sides the alloy escutcheons from their own issue sun helmet; these followed the design of the steel helmet decals. A photo of the renowned Ofw.Barlesius, who first scouted the British advance at the start of Wavell's Operation 'Battleaxe', shows that in this reconnaissance unit of 15.Panzer-Division the men also added to their headgear the 'dragoon eagle' or '*Schwedter Adler*'. This bronze Prussian eagle was one of three authorised tradition badges worn by German Army units in commemoration of old German regiments: in this case, Aufkl.Abt.33 was formed from personnel of Reiter-Regiment 6, some squadrons of which were allowed to wear the

Oberst Gerhard Müller of the DAK, awarded the Knight's Cross on 15 September 1942, and photographed here in the full tropical uniform of a Panzer colonel. The tropical field cap is piped silver for commissioned rank, and bears the pink soutache identifying arm-of-service. The open-collar olive tunic bears the collar Litzen and shoulder straps common to both tropical and Continental field grey uniform, the arm-of-service marked by the addition of the Panzer skulls from the vehicle uniform patches to the lower lapels. Breast decorations are the Iron Cross 1st Class which Müller won in the First World War, below the silver eagle pin marking a second award in the Second World War; a Wound Badge; and the General Assault Badge. (ECPA)

Typical tank crew of the Deutsches Afrika Korps, wearing olive shirts and shorts and a mixture of tropical field caps and the black Feldmütze. A captured South African Army sun helmet is slung on the turret; and note long desert boots. (ECPA)

eagle between the national eagle and the cockade on all headgear in memory of the old 1st Brandenburg Dragoons.

The tropical shirt was issued in a dark sand yellow shade, but quickly faded. It had four small buttons on the 'pullover' front, uniform buttons on the pockets, another pair on the shoulders for attachment of conventional shoulder straps, and box-pleated chest pockets. The shorts were issued in the same olive material as the tunic and trousers. A short version of the composite desert boot was issued, worn with ankle socks. A surviving cap from this unit shows yellow cavalry *Waffenfarbe*, which is therefore shown on the shoulder straps of this figure.

D2: Feldwebel, Panzer-Regiment 8; Libya, 1941–42
Panzer personnel wore the same tropical uniforms as other branches of the *Deutsches Afrika Korps*. The tropical field cap was apparently worn mainly by vehicle crews, as the peaked tropical cap was found inconvenient in the confines of a tank. Like all other parts of the uniform it was made in a dull olive-khaki, but faded out (or was deliberately bleached) to any number of paler shades of green, brown or yellow. On both the caps and the tropical tunic the national eagle was in light blue on a brown backing, and the cockade was also woven on brown. The V of pink piping was worn as on Continental uniform caps. The collar and shoulder straps of NCOs from Unteroffizier upwards were distinguished by *Tresse*, but in a copper-brown shade rather than silver. Collar *Litzen* in light blue on brown were worn by all non-commissioned ranks, and in Panzer units the skulls from the collar patches of the black vehicle uniform were pinned directly to the lower lapels. Only these, and the outer piping of the shoulder straps, identify branch. The long, loose trousers are gathered by tapes over brown laced ankle-boots. Olive web belts were issued to the DAK, with the normal buckle painted over with green. The 'Afrikakorps' cuff title was normally but not always worn on this uniform.

D3: Oberleutnant, Panzer-Regiment 8; Libya, 1942

The tropical field cap was both practical and stylish. Made of olive drill, it was often deliberately bleached to a pale sandy shade. National insignia were as for the sidecap (D1); officers sometimes replaced the light blue eagle with one in silver on brown, and the flat-woven cockade with a raised boss in black, silver and red; equally often they did not bother, and retained the enlisted ranks' insignia. Officers' caps with silver crown-seam piping, and sometimes with silver piping in the front scallop of the false turn-up, were common; again, many officers wore the issue cap. The tropical tunic was the same for all ranks, and most officers seem to have retained the light blue eagle, although some replaced it with the silver-on-black or silver-on-dark-green eagles from their black or field grey Continental uniforms. Buttons were supposed to be olive-painted, but many photos show them scrubbed silver. Shoulder straps were exactly as for the Continental uniforms. Collar *Litzen* from the field grey service uniform were worn on the upper collar, and in armoured units the patch-skulls were pinned to the lower lapel. An alternative to the loose slacks were these semi-breeches in various shades of olive, worn by all ranks. The high canvas and leather desert boots were also worn irrespective of rank, according to taste and availability.

E1: Panzerschütze, schwere Panzer-Abteilung 503; Normandy, 1944

The black *Einheitsfeldmütze* for Panzer troops was introduced in 1943, but the sidecap—*Feldmütze*—continued to be worn alongside it until the end of the war. The national eagle, in mouse grey, and the cockade were woven together on a wedge-shaped black backing and sewn to the crown. Photos of this Corps heavy tank battalion, which fought in Normandy with Tiger E and Königstiger tanks, show a small silver pin in the shape of a Tiger tank on the left side of the turn-up, a typical example of the unofficial insignia sometimes acquired and worn at unit level in 1944–45. From about 1943 very dark grey shirts become more common in photos of armoured personnel. The 'reed green Panzer drill uniform' was introduced as working dress and hot-weather combat dress from about mid-1942. Because it was authorised as a uniform in its own right, not merely as working denims, it was often embellished with collar patches, battle badges and decorations. It was cut almost identically to the black vehicle uniform, but may be distinguished from the armoured car denims by the large left-thigh pocket, and often by a large external pocket on the left chest. The sleeve rank patches (see F5, H3) were often applied.

E2: Schütze, Panzer-Aufklärungs-Abteiling 115; Italy, summer 1944

Camouflage-printed uniforms were not a general issue to Panzer troops. However, individual officers purchased a variety of camouflage jackets in German Army 'splinter' and 'water' patterns, in Waffen-SS pattern, and in Italian camouflage cloth; and photos show some use of denim suits or overalls in the latter material worn by enlisted ranks. After the 1943 armistice and the German occupation of Italy large stocks of the Italian material, in a pattern of leaf green, chestnut brown and straw yellow, were seized; and we base this painting on photos of an armoured car crewman of this unit. Quantities of this material are also seen in photos taken in Normandy. The cut of these camouflage denims varied considerably; this example, interestingly enough, shows a particularly 'Italian' feature in that the doubling or yoke of material over the shoulders and upper chest is cut at the front to incorporate the breast pocket flaps, in the style of the Italian *sahariana* jacket. A seam across the back at the same level is cut in three points. Such overalls were worn alone in hot weather, or over the black uniform in cold weather.

E3: Panzershütze; Normandy, 1944

The chaotic mixture of denim outfits worn by armoured personnel in the last two years of the war often led to different outfits being worn within the same crew. There was no assured supply of any particular set; and Panzer troops are often seen wearing the 'universal' denim uniform introduced as hot-weather combat dress for the Army as a whole in summer 1942. This was a light-weight copy of the field service dress, with a four-pocket tunic and straight trousers. Photos show Panzer men wearing it with the tunic skirt tucked into the trousers, and the belt passed through the front belt-loops, as here. The normal field service collar *Litzen* and the national eagle were applied in mouse grey on greenish field grey backing. Again, pocket layout allows photographic identification. The *Waffenfarbe* cap piping is seen in individual cases right up to 1945, although ordered out of use in September 1942. The shoulder straps of the black uniform were often worn with these denims.

F1: Oberst Graf Strachwitz, Panzer-Regiment 'Grossdeutschland'; Russia, March 1943

A number of personal styles of headgear and clothing were adopted against the cold of the Russian winter by officers and men. The regulation officer's greatcoat was often modified by adding fur or fleece collar-facing, as here. A wide range of fur, fleece, or part-cloth, part-fur caps were used; this modification of the black Panzer officer's *Feldmütze* by the addition of black astrakhan fleece to the turn-up is particularly striking, and seems to be unique in the known photographs. One may guess that its dapper appearance caused humorous comment; but the fear of being laughed at would hardly deter an officer who went on to win the Oakleaves and Swords to the Knight's Cross, and to command the Panzer-Lehr-Division—a man, moreover, who had already survived the experience of being christened Hyazinth Graf Strachwitz von Gross-Zauche und Camminetz . . .

F2: Generalmajor Adalbert Schultz, 7.Panzer-Division; Russia, January 1944

This officer, killed in action shortly after assuming command of his division, was unusual in that he is seen in photos wearing general officer's collar patches in gold and red attached to the black vehicle uniform; normally the usual pink-piped skull patches were worn by all ranks. (Another officer described as following this unauthorised practice was Generalleutnant Hoppe of the 278.Volksgrenadier-Division.) Panzer generals wore gold in place of silver piping on the black officer's *Feldmütze*, and a gold national eagle on both cap and jacket. Schultz wears his *Ritterkreuz* with *Eichenlaub* and *Schwerten* at the throat.

Excellent portrait of Major von Wietersheim, commander in 1943 of the Pz-Regt. 'Grossdeutschland'; note silver cord twist piping on officer's-pattern black Feldmütze, and gilt 'GD' cypher pinned to the shoulder straps. (Bundesarchiv)

F3: Oberst, Panzertruppe; Italy, summer 1944

In Italy a wide variety of both Continental and tropical uniform items was worn by German troops of all branches and ranks. A photo of this unidentified officer shows a particularly interesting and uncharacteristic combination, in that the tropical tunic, dyed to a very pale shade, is embellished by the addition of the skull patches from the black vehicle uniform. Conventional shoulder straps of rank and branch are, untypically, sewn permanently to the tunic, as is the silver and black Panzer officer's breast eagle. In the buttonhole is the ribbon of the First World War Iron Cross, with the silver device marking a second award after 1939. The 'Afrika' commemorative cuff title is worn on the left forearm, and the last item on the ribbon bar can be identified as the Italian-German Medal for that campaign. The headgear is the regulation *Schirmmütze* of the Continental service uniform, with silver officer's cords and pink Panzer piping.

F4: Oberst Erich Schmidt, schwere Panzer-Abteilung 507; Russia, 1944

This commander of a Corps Tiger unit wears the 'old style officer's field cap', an alternative to the *Schirmmütze* much favoured by Panzer officers since its smaller and unstiffened shape was handier inside armoured vehicles. Of the same basic colours, it bore silver-on-dark-green insignia woven flat on cloth patches; the peak was of semi-stiff leather, and no cords were worn (although in individual cases one sees them added). The mouse grey shirt was seen in many shades; field grey and dark charcoal grey versions were often worn, and private-purchase black shirts were not unknown. Here it displays the maximum of insignia and decorations. Below a silver-on-black eagle is the cloth version of the War Order of the German Cross in Gold. The Knight's Cross is worn at the throat, the Iron Cross 1st Class, silver Wound Badge, and Panzer Battle Badge on the chest. Shoulder straps are buttoned and looped in place.

F5: Major, Panzer-Regiment 16; Lorraine, autumn 1944

This officer, tentatively identified as Major Graf von Brühl, commander of the 2nd Bn. of the tank regiment of 116.Panzer-Division, wears the officer's version of the black *Einheitsfeldmütze* with regulation silver insignia and seam-piping. The photo we copy shows on the left side the small black and silver pin bearing the division's 'Windhund' insignia, widely worn by all ranks of this formation. The tunic is made from Italian camouflage material, and is a typical privately acquired combat garment. On the left upper arm is the major's rank patch—two oak-sprays and a bar in green, on black—from the sequence authorised in August 1942 for wear on all garments which did not display rank on shoulder straps or collar patches: in the armoured units, this included the reed green Panzer denims, snow camouflage garments, printed camouflage garments, etc.

G1: Gefreiter, Sturmartillerie; France, 1941

A photo showing a unit of Assault Artillery apparently training with captured French equipment provides us with this combination of items typical of the confusion attending Sturmartillerie uniform in this period. The black Panzer *Schutzmütze* is worn with the field grey vehicle uniform. This bears normal shoulder straps and rank chevron, and the field grey collar patches piped red.

Major, Aufklärungs-Abteilung 33, wearing the 'Schwedter-Adler' dragoon tradition badge on his field grey Feldmütze. See Plate G2 for discussion of this uniform.

G2: Major, Panzer-Aufklärungs-Abteilung 33; 1944

Taken from a well-known and interesting portrait of a *Ritterkreuzträger* reproduced on this page. Photos from 1943–45 show increased use of the field grey vehicle uniform in armoured reconnaissance units in place of the original black uniform, although the change was by no means universal. It is worth noting that even APC-borne Panzer-Grenadiers were sometimes photographed so uniformed in 1944–45. A question is raised by the colour of the *Waffenfarbe*. Officially it should have been pink, with 'A' cyphers on the shoulder straps, by this period. But no cyphers are visible; and the continued use of the 'dragoon eagle' badge reminds us of the strong cavalry traditions of this unit. I have chosen to speculate that cavalry yellow *Waffenfarbe* is still worn here, but am subject to correction. The photo does not extend downwards to show the sleeve, but given the deployment of this unit and the officer's rank and decorations the 'Afrika' cuff title is a fair assumption—no desert veteran would willingly forego this prestigious insignia. The Winter 1941 ribbon is worn in the buttonhole beneath the Honour Roll Clasp on a strip of Iron Cross 2nd Class ribbon; and high on the left chest is the Close Combat Bar.

G3: Leutnant, Sturmgeschütz-Brigade 276; East Prussia, November 1944

One of the officers from the group photograph mentioned in the 'Uniforms' section of the text, wearing a not-uncommon combination of items for the late war period. The conventional artillery officer's *Schirmmütze* is unstiffened and 'operational' in appearance. Roll-neck sweaters of grey and, less often, black were often worn with the vehicle uniform in combat. The black uniform bears conventional collar *Litzen* with artillery-red 'lights'.

G4: Major, Sturmgeschütz-Abteilung 249(?); 1944–45

The subject photo shows shoulder strap cyphers ending in '49' attached temporarily by grey cloth loops; since this is the only Sturmartillerie unit listed with a number ending with these digits, we speculate accordingly. The officer's 1943 *Einheitsfeldmütze* is silver-piped and has silver insignia. The field grey uniform is conventional, apart from the addition of the Jäger patch to the right sleeve, suggesting that this unit was attached to a Jäger-Division.

G5: Hauptmann, Sturmartillerie, 1945

The bulky headset was replaced in some cases by the issue, from late 1944, of the improved *Kopfhaube A* set; this had the earphones set low on the pads, allowing them to be worn under a steel helmet. Ironically, by the time the new headset appeared, shortages of helmets had led to their no longer being standard issue to armoured units. The odd combination of items on this uniform—pink-piped collar and 'empty' patches on the black Panzer uniform—is discussed in the 'Uniforms' section of the text. It was apparently quite widely worn by Sturmartillerie personnel in 1943–45.

H1: Major Dr. Franz Bäke; Russia 1943–44

This gallant officer commanded Panzer-Regiment 11 in 6.Panzer-Division in 1943–44. Early in 1944 he was given command of an *ad hoc* heavy intervention regiment under I Panzer-Armee. This was made up of the remaining Tigers of sPz-Abt.503, a Panther battalion, some SP artillery and an engineer unit. Panzer-Regiment Bäke greatly distinguished themselves in a number of desperate actions. In one five-day battle at the 'Balabonowka Pocket' they destroyed 267 Soviet tanks for a (carefully checked and confirmed) loss of just one Tiger and four Panthers. Bäke was awarded the Swords to his Knight's Cross with Oakleaves, and commanded the 13.Panzer-Division ('Feldherrnhalle 2') in the last days of the war, with colonel's rank.

He wears a black 1943 *Einheitsfeldmütze* with a substantial silver-wire eagle but apparently no cockade. This cannot be hidden under the turn-up, since this is sewn down and an unauthorised (but not uncommon) length of silver piping is added to its front scallop, in addition to the regulation crown-seam piping. The jacket retains pink collar piping; the patches are conventional, as are the shoulder straps. Among the insignia on the left chest is a gold Wound Badge, signifying five or more wounds in action. Further proof of Bäke's personal heroism is provided by the three Individual Tank Destruction Badges on his right sleeve. These were awarded, it must be emphasised, for the single-handed destruction of an enemy tank with hand-held weapons or explosives, and not for fighting from an armoured vehicle. Unusually placed in the lower lapel buttonhole are the ribbon of the Winter 1941 Medal, and the 1914 Iron Cross with 1939 bar.

H2: Generalmajor Mäder, Führer-Grenadier-Division; Eastern Front, 1944–45

A photo of this divisional commander, whose formation qualified for the cuff title 'Grossdeutschland' by being included in the expanded Korps of that name, shows this interesting combination of

A dashing young Oberstleutnant of the Pz-Regt.'GD' wearing the silver-piped officer's pattern 1943 Einheitsfeldmütze, and a grey roll-neck sweater in place of a shirt. (ECPA)

the field grey Sturmartillerie jacket, the general officer's red and gold collar patches, and the general officer's red-striped breeches. The cap is speculative, but in the last stages of the war many generals adopted a version of the *Einheitsfeldmütze* with gold piping and insignia.

H3: Major Willy Jähde, schwere Panzer-Abteilung 502; Russia, early 1944

A photo shows this combination of regulation and private-purchase items. The black *Feldmütze* is still worn, with silver officer's piping, but without the pink *soutache* by this date. The black vehicle uniform is covered by cold-weather clothing; the jacket, with unpiped collar, is fastened across to the throat, and the Knight's Cross is worn under its collar. Over this Jähde wears a personally-acquired coat of dark natural sheepskin, fleece inside; it has no collar, but a tab apparently buttons to the right across the throat when the zip is pulled up. On the left sleeve he wears the authorised rank patch. The bottom half of the padded, reversible winter camouflage suit issued to the German Army in winter 1942–43 is worn white side outermost. Note that the legs were rather short, and draw-stringed tightly over the boots.

Select Bibliography

General works on German Army uniform:

Davis, B. L., *German Army Uniforms and Insignia 1933–45*, Arms & Armour Press

Davis, B. L., *German Uniforms of the Third Reich 1933–45*, Blandford Press

Various, *Uniformes Hors-Serie No. 1: La Wehrmacht*, Argout-Editions

Armoured unit history, uniform and equipment:

Bender, R. J. & Odegard, W. W., *Uniforms, Organisation and History of the Panzertruppe*, R. James Bender Publishing

Bender, R. J. & Law, R. D., *Uniforms, Organisation and History of the Afrikakorps*, R. James Bender Publishing

Macksey, K., *Panzer Division*, Pan-Ballantine

Perrett, B., *Sturmartillerie and Panzerjäger (Vanguard 12)*, Osprey Publishing

Perrett, B., *The Panzerkampfwagen III (Vgd. 16)*, Osprey Publishing

Perrett, B., *The Panzerkampfwagen IV (Vgd. 18)*, Osprey Publishing

Perrett, B., *The Tiger Tanks (Vgd. 20)*, Osprey Publishing

Perrett, B., *The PzKpfw V Panther (Vgd. 21)*, Osprey Publishing

Perrett, B., *German Armoured Cars and Reconnaissance Half-Tracks (Vgd. 25)*, Osprey Publishing

Other German armoured units:

Bender, R. J. & Taylor, H. P., *Uniforms, Organisation and History of the Waffen-SS, Vols. 1, 2 & 3*, R. James Bender Publishing

Bender, R. J. & Petersen, G. A., *'Hermann Göring': from Regiment to Fallschirmpanzerkorps*, R. James Bender Publishing

Quarrie, B., *Fallschirmpanzerdivision 'Hermann Göring' (Vgd. 4)*, Osprey Publishing

Windrow, M. C., *The Waffen-SS (Revised Edition) (Men-at-Arms 34 Revised)*, Osprey Publishing

INDEX

(References to illustrations are shown in **bold**. Plates are shown with caption locators in brackets.)